Bristol Radical Pampl

The Maltreat__ ___
the Malcontents

Working in the Great Western Cotton Factory
1838-1914

Mike Richardson

ISBN 978-1-911522-36-2

Bristol Radical History Group. 2016.
www.brh.org.uk
brh@brh.org.uk

Contents

Acknowledgements

Sheila Rowbotham, comrade and partner. I couldn't have written this without your editorial insight and support. The Bristol Radical History Group for encouragement and commitment to publish history from below. Richard Grove for his work on the cover design and photographs, and the University of the West of England for the use of their facilities in my standing as a Visiting Research Fellow.

Images/Text are reproduced with the kind permission of The British Newspaper Archive (www.britishnewspaperarchive.co.uk), and Local World Limited and the Bristol Record Office. For quotes and references to nineteenth century British newspapers; Text © THE BRITISH LIBRARY BOARD. ALL RIGHTS RESERVED. In respect to the *Western Daily Press* and *Bristol Times and Mirror*, text are reproduced with the kind permission of both The British Newspaper Archive and the Bristol Central Reference Library. The *Felix Farley Journal* with permission from the Bristol Central Reference Library alone.

Mike Baker's Barton Hill History Group Sign on one of the few buildings that remain from the Great Western Cotton Works.

Picture Credits

For permission to reproduce pictures from Bristol Records Office (BRO) please contact bro@bristol.gov.uk and for those from Bristol Central Reference Library contact refandinfo@bristol.gov.uk.

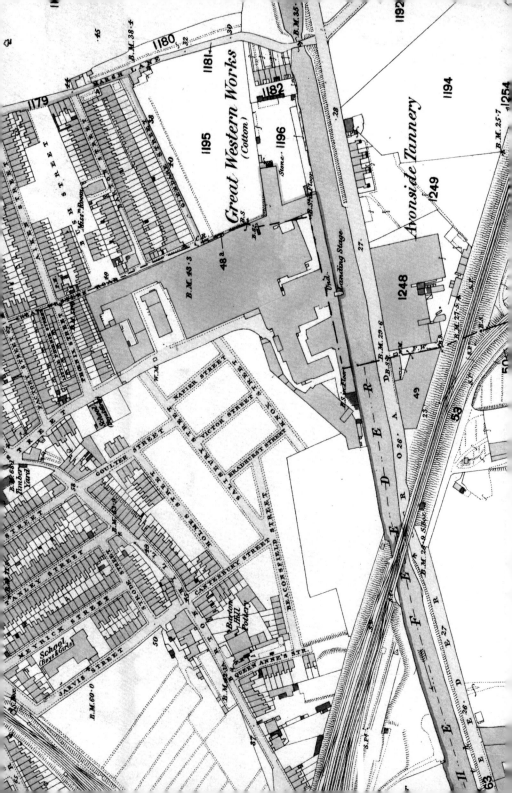

Introduction

Bristol's contribution to the English textile industry in the Victorian and Edwardian era has received little attention,[1] and virtually nothing has been published on the trials and tribulations of its workforce.[2] It is understandable that given Lancashire's dominance in the production of cotton goods historians have focused on the North. Nevertheless, the numbers employed in Bristol's Great Western Cotton Works (a spinning and weaving factory) soon came to be equal in size to some of the largest cotton mills in Manchester.[3] An exploration of the conditions and experiences of Bristol's cotton operatives is overdue. My account is informed by the approach of the Bristol Radical History Group - history from below.

Britain in the 1830s was in a period of transition. Fundamental social, economic and political change was underway. Voices representing the poor and dispossessed emerged railing against injustice and the bleak conditions endured by factory workers. In an address to their sisters of the West of England and South Wales in 1839 the Committee of the Bristol Female Patriotic Association (supporters of the People's Charter, 1838)[4] declared

> we have learned by bitter experience that slavery is not confined to colour or clime - that even in England cruel oppression reigns. We have seen the earnings of our husbands inadequate to the support of his family - we have seen the wife compelled to leave her home neglected, and with her infant children, work at a soul-and-body-degrading toil, to make up the loss sustained by legal robbery. ... But, dear sisters, if it was just and laudable to enlist our sympathy, and secure our co-operation, in the cause of negro emancipation, it must be our interest, as well as our duty, to aid in our own enfranchisement from a state of worse than Egyptian bondage.[5]

1 See S. Jones, 'The Cotton Industry in Bristol', *Transactions and Papers (Institute of British Geographers)*, No. 13 (1947).
2 The only exceptions are M. Richardson, 'The Bristol Strike Wave of 1889-90: Socialists, New Unionists and New Women: Part 1: Days of Hope' in D. Backwith, R. Ball, S. E. Hunt and M. Richardson (eds), *Strikers, Hobblers, Conchies and Reds: A Radical History of Bristol 1880-1939* (London: Breviary Stuff Publications, 2014) and G. Atterton, *Cotton Threads: The History of the Great Western Cotton Factory* (Bristol: Barton Hill History Group, June 2015).
3 H. Jennings, *Societies in the Making: A Study of Development and Redevelopment within a County Borough* (London: Routledge & Kegan Paul, 1962), p. 31.
4 The People's Charter was a public petition containing six demands, including the enfranchisement of men aged twenty-one and over and annual parliaments, to reform the electoral system with the objective of addressing the interests of the working classes who wanted employment and decent wages to feed their families.
5 Address of the Bristol Female Patriotic Association signed by the Committee (Mrs Lloyd, Mrs Rice, Mrs Mathews, Mrs Lewis, Miss M. Taylor, Mrs Chevers, Treasurer, Miss Taylor, Secretary) on their behalf, to their sisters of the West of England and South Wales, *Northern Star*, 3 August 1839, p. 6.

It was not uncommon for early nineteenth century workers to describe their labour in terms of slavery. The comparison was not simply figurative but inscribed in material life and culture.

The Bristol riots of 1831 haunted the city's top brass when in an explosion of anger the lower orders rebelled, ransacking and burning the houses of the wealthy and politically corrupt. The fury of the crowd had made it apparent to Bristol's ruling elite that unless the grievances of the working class were addressed the masses would remain embittered and thus pose a threat to the existing state of affairs. Anxiety about the possibility of another outbreak of social unrest preoccupied the Bristol middle classes. In November and December 1837, the *Bristol Mercury* published a series of letters debating the efficacy of the Poor Law Amendment Act (1834) and the condition and prospects of the working classes.[6]

Discomfort about the plight of the working class, however, did not hinder the law from its determination to proceed against those accused of riot. In early April 1838, several years after his involvement in the Bristol uprisings, Thomas Lanny was sentenced to death.[7] The death penalty served those desirous of revenge but masked the root cause of what was ailing Bristol's poor. Therefore, those troubled about the extent and consequences of unemployment and poverty welcomed the fact that a cotton factory was in the process of construction in Bristol and 'would afford employment to a great number of persons, and clear the streets of unemployed children.'[8]

The spectacular growth of the textile industry had powered Britain's industrial revolution. By 1835 the British cotton industry employed 258,545 workers, predominately women and children, a significant number of these worked in large mechanized mills in Lancashire and to a lesser extent in the Glasgow-Paisley district.[9] The relative decline of Bristol's economy compared with the ascendency of other major provincial ports such as Liverpool and Glasgow triggered, somewhat belatedly, the search for new avenues of industrial growth. One alternative source of profit under consideration was that of producing cotton products on an industrial scale. Britain's political control over territories [such as India] had provided a protected market for the British

6 *Bristol Mercury*, 11 & 25 November 1837 and 9, 16 & 23 December 1837.
7 *Worcestershire Chronicle*, 12 April 1838, p. 4.
8 J. B. Clarke, managing director of Clarke, Acramans, Maze and Co., *Bristol Mercury*, 22 July 1837, p. 3.
9 J. Greenlees, *Female Labour Power: Women Workers' Influence in Business Practices in British and American Cotton Industries, 1780-1860* (Aldershot: Ashgate, 2007) p. 26; A. E. Musson, *The Growth of British Industry* (London: Batsford, paperback edition, 1981) p. 82.

textile industry.[10] However, the case for launching a cotton mill in Bristol to rival those in Lancashire and Scotland had not attracted serious attention until after both the slave trade, and slavery, were abolished under the Acts of 1807 and 1833.

In the early nineteenth century, finance for infrastructure and new enterprise in the city was largely derived from the profits made by Bristol merchants in the slave trade during the seventeenth and eighteenth centuries.[11] However, following the 1833 Act it was the significant amount of compensation paid to slave-owners, £20 million (in relation to the size of the economy, this would be equivalent to around £76 billion today)[12] for the loss of their 'property' by the British government, which in substantially enhancing the personal wealth of former slave-holders enabled them to invest in established and new ventures. Bristol recipients of compensation shifted their interest away from the West India trade, staking their capital elsewhere. Some of this investment found its way into the local economy[13] and was used to help finance the building of the Great Western Railway and the Great Western Cotton Company.

In April 1837 several former Bristol mercantile slave-holders entered into partnership with the Manchester cotton manufacturer, Joseph Bell Clarke, and others, under the firm of Clarke, Acramans, Maze and Company.[14] This newly formed partnership put up the initial capital for building and equipping a cotton mill in Barton Hill, part of the out-parish of St. Philip and St. Jacob on the banks of the Feeder Canal, and presumed primary responsibility for its long-term financing.

Much of this capital, however, was tainted, as seven of the firm's fifteen partners, Thomas Kington, George Gibbs, Robert Bright, Charles Pinney, Robert Edward Case, George Henry Ames, and Henry Bush, had received a considerable amount of compensation as slave-owners, while those that had been enslaved received nothing.[15] Another partner with strong Bristol connections, Philip William Skynner (P.W.S.) Miles, benefited from the legacy of British

10 S. Beckert, *Empire of Cotton: A New History of Global Capitalism* (London: Penguin, 2014), p. 310.
11 Jones, 'The Cotton Industry in Bristol', p. 72.
12 N. Draper, *The Price of Emancipation: Slave-ownership, Compensation and British Society at the End of Slavery* (Cambridge: Cambridge University Press, 2013, first published 2010), p. 107.
13 P. Marshall, *Bristol and the Abolition of Slavery: The Politics of Emancipation* (Bristol: Bristol Branch of the Historical Association, Pamphlet No. 37, 1975), p. 27.
14 Jones, 'The Cotton Industry in Bristol', pp. 73-4.
15 *Legacies of British Slave-Ownership* (London: UCL Department of History 2015, https://www.ucl.ac.uk/lbs/ accessed 31 May 2015); Deed of Partnership of the Great Western Cotton Company, February 28 1837, Bristol Record Office.

Aerial View of The Great Western Cotton Works, 1926.

slave-ownership through his grandfather, William, and his father, Philip John, whose compensation as a slave-owner amounted to almost £50,000.[16] Moreover, when the company was formed in 1837 eight of its partners were serving members of the Town Council (seven Conservatives and two Liberals) which had been established following the passing of the 1835 Municipal Corporations Act, and one, P.W.S. Miles, was a Member of Parliament (MP) for the Bristol Constituency.

The building of the cotton works just outside the Bristol city boundary was a gigantic undertaking. Four hundred and fifty local artisans and labourers were used for its construction, including the erection of a tall octagon chimney.[17] On completion in April 1838[18] the factory, which from 1838 to 1845 became known as Clarke, Maze and Company, Great Western Cotton Works, comprised five floors, each sixty feet wide, 300 feet long, and between twelve and fourteen feet high. Over 900 windows provided natural light. The whole of the establishment was said to be fireproof. Powered by two steam engines of eighty horsepower each, and six fifty-horsepower boilers, the factory had the capacity to produce between 160,000 and 180,000 yards of coarse calico per week from a 1,000 power looms contained in a 250 by 350 feet weaving room.[19] A large proportion of the looms and other machinery was made and repaired on site. The works' foundry cast the iron for the making and repair of these machines.[20]

While the materials and labour required for the assemblage of the cotton mill depended on capital derived from slave-compensation, its operation hinged on a labour force predominately made up of children and young adults on low wages and slave-based produce - cotton from America - in order to compete with the well-established Lancashire textile industry.

---

16 C. Hall, N. Draper, K. McCelland, K. Donington and R. Lang, *Legacies of British Slave-ownership: Colonial Slavery and the Formation of Victorian Britain* (Cambridge: Cambridge University Press, 2014), p. 135.

17 *Felix Farley's Journal*, 21 April 1838.

18 *Bristol Mercury*, 21 April 1838, p. 4. The opening of the Bristol's cotton factory took place in the same year that five members of a secret association of Glasgow operative cotton spinners were charged with conspiracy and murder during an 'illegal' cotton workers strike. Four of the men were subsequently found guilty of conspiracy (the murder charge was not proven) and sentenced to seven years transportation. A petition from the Bristol Working Men's Association called on the House of Commons to request the Queen for a free pardon for the men, *Northern Star*, 27 January 1838, p. 6. The men were finally pardoned in 1840.

19 *Morning Post*, 10 September 1838, p. 2.

20 *Western Daily Press*, 3 April 1930, p. 7. The original St. Philip's Street Bridge (a toll bridge), near Temple Meads, was cast and put together by the Great Western Cotton Company in 1841.

Street signs around the site of the Great Western Cotton Works in Barton Hill. Maze Street, Aiken Street and Great Western Lane (as Road) date to the time of the factory, Cotton Mill Lane is a modern addition. The building behind the Cotton Mill Lane sign, and at the bottom right of Great Western Lane, is one of the few remnants of the factory visible today.

Many of the children working in the early English textile mills were regularly beaten and flogged. One example of their harsh and cruel treatment was captured in the testimony of a ten-year-old girl, Ellen Hootton, given to His Majesty's Factory Inquiry Commission in June 1833. She reported that her overlooker frequently hit her. And in one incident she recalled how she had iron weights strapped to her back and made to walk around the throstle spinning room 'with a cap on her head and a stick in her hand'. The point of the punishment was to shame her in front of the other children.[21]

Freedom to walk away from the job was restricted. Under the 1823 British Master and Servant Act to breach the employment contract was, until 1875 when it was repealed, a criminal offence. The enforcement of this coercive contract was a way to remedy insubordination, stop workers from withdrawing their labour without proper notice, go absent without permission, or simply

21 D. A. Galbi, 'Through Eyes in the Storm: Aspects of the Personal History of Women Workers in the Industrial Revolution', *Social History* Vol. 21 No. 2 May 1996, p. 143, 147, 151 & 152.

leave for another job with higher wages. Under the Master and Servant law employees too could summon employers for unpaid wages and ill-treatment, although it 'offered only civil remedies when employers violated agreements.'[22] Thus employers who appeared before the magistrates were not treated as criminals, while workers accused of breach of contract would be apprehended and placed under arrest.

In the eyes of the law, the liberal idea of equality between the seller and buyer of labour power was remote from the actual experience of textile workers who did not require theoretical lessons from a biased legal system on exploitation. During the period 1855-75, 'between at least 7,300 and 17,000 workers a year were prosecuted for breach of contract in England' under Master and Servants Acts. The impact of these Acts served to tighten the shackles of workers' dependency, thereby easing the ability of employers to keep wages down and profits up.[23]

The vast majority of the Great Western cotton workers struggled to survive on the wages they received. While selling their labour power in order to purchase the means of existence, many of them would have been aware that they produced more value to their capitalist employer than the amount he paid them. Moreover, the huge gap between what they were paid and the rewards their employers and managers received fuelled their discontent. Many considered the compensation they received in wages for their labour was unfair and unjust. A sense of injustice together with the ongoing battle to provide enough food for themselves and those dependent upon their earnings was the root cause of resentment.[24]

22 C. Frank, *Master and Servant Law: Chartists, Trade Unions, Radical Lawyers and the Magistracy in England, 1840-1865* (Aldershot: Ashgate, 2010) p. 2; D. Hay, and P. Craven, 'Master and Servant in England and the Empire: A Comparative Study', Labour/Le Travail, 31, 1993, p. 175.

23 Frank, *Master and Servant Law: Chartists, Trade Unions, Radical Lawyers and the Magistracy in England, 1840-1865*, p.5.

24 The secret of profit-making emerging out of the sale and purchase of labour power is analyzed in K. Marx, *Capital: A Critique of Political Economy*, Vol. One, Chapter Six, 'The Sale and Purchase of Labour-Power (London: Penguin, 1976), pp. 270-280.

Part 1 The 1830s and 1840s

Chapter 1

Child Labour Laws and Regulating the Poor

By the time the Great Western Cotton Works was built significant legislative changes had begun to affect the institutional framework of both labour conditions and poor relief. Agitation for factory reform, and pressure for restraint upon the unbridled drive for profit, came from several differing sources. John Doherty, an Irish born trade union leader, was the principal voice of the male cotton spinners in Manchester and an ardent supporter of the Ten-Hour movement, led by Lord Ashley (Anthony Ashley-Cooper, later the 7th Earl of Shaftesbury) and the Tory radicals Richard Oastler and Michael Sadler.[25] Oastler was known by his contemporaries to be a ' Church and King tory of the old sort'.[26] He was one of

> the romantic Tories, whose soul rebelled against capitalism which, with cynical callousness, was turning the "good old" England upside down and bringing material and moral disintegration into the historic life-forms of the people and of society.[27]

Sadler was also concerned about the destruction of traditional society. He was a benevolent Tory statesman moved by his sense of duty to God to support in his words the 'maltreated, outraged, and over-laboured' and under-paid workers exploited by employers, 'often from the lower ranks of the community, who 'became suddenly and immensely rich.'[28]

It was Sadler, a Member of Parliament for Leeds, who chaired a Committee of investigation into conditions of work in the factories. This Committee published a report in August 1832 that exposed the horror stories of factory life in textile mills. Sadler, however, lost his parliamentary seat in the 1832 election and his proposal, moved by Ashley, for a ten-hour day for all workers under eighteen was defeated.

25 S. & B. Webb, *History of Trade Unionism* (London: Longmans, 1920), pp. 117-8, ftn. 2.

26 A. S. Kydd, *The History of the Factory Movement from the year 1802*, to the Enactment of the Ten Hour Bill in 1847, Vol. 1 (London: Simpkin, Marshall and Co., 1857), p. 104.

27 T. Rothstein, *From Chartism to Labourism: Historical Sketches of the English Working Class Movement* (London: Lawrence and Wishart, 1983, first published in 1929), p. 54.

28 Kydd, *The History of the Factory Movement from the year 1802, to the Enactment of the Ten Hour Bill in 1847*, Vol. 2, p. 17.

However, pressure from below could not be ignored. When Government commissioners went to Leeds in 1832 to gather information on conditions of work in the factories, hundreds of children lobbied the commissioners with the ditty:

We will have the Ten Hours Bill
    That we will, that we will;
Or the land shall ne'er be still,
    Ne'er be still, ne'er be still;
Parliament say what they will,
    WE WILL HAVE THE TEN HOURS BILL[29]

In 1833, the momentum for state regulation of industrial employment led to the passing of (Viscount) Althorp's Factory Act, named after the Leader of the House of Commons. This Act subjected the employment of child labour in textile factories (except silk) to standards set by parliament. The 1833 Factory Act stipulated that no children were to work in textile mills under the age of nine. Children aged between nine and thirteen were limited to working nine hours per day or forty-eight hours per week. The Act also required children under thirteen to receive two hours' schooling on six days a week. Early reports by factory inspectors, however, indicated that some employers were circumventing the law.[30] While in its first few years of operation there is no evidence that the owners of the Great Western Cotton Works flouted this Act, the fear of being discharged would have discouraged most factory hands from submitting any official complaints.[31] Moreover, the omission of setting up the machinery to enforce this Act amounted 'to nothing more than a barren declaration of principles' making it easy for textile employers to disregard legislation if they so wished.[32]

To satisfy its demand for child labour the Great Western Cotton Company did resort to employing pauper children on low wages from the local workhouse; a practice that contravened the 1834 Poor Law Amendment Act. Correspondence between the chairman of the Board of Guardians of the Clifton New Poor Law Union and the secretary of the Poor-Law Commission, Edwin Chadwick, indicated that some pauper children from the St. Philip and

29 Cited in D. Thompson, *The British People 1760-1902* (London: Heinemann Educational, 1969), p. 104.
30 C. Nardinelli, 'Child Labor and the Factory Acts', *The Journal of Economic History*, Vol. 40, No. 4 (Dec. 1980), p. 743.
31 F. Engels, *The Condition of the Working Class in England in Karl Marx, Frederick Engels Collected Works* Vol. 4 (London: Lawrence & Wishart, 1975), p. 460.
32 E. Halévy, *A History of the English People in the Nineteenth Century* Vol. 3 (London: Benn, 1961), p. 108.

St. Jacob's workhouse were employed at the mill for several months after its opening in 1838. The Commissioners stepped in to stop this practice on the grounds that *'persons receiving relief* [under the 1834 Poor Law Amendment Act] *shall not enter into competition with persons supporting themselves by their own labour'* (Italics in original), unless 'the owner of the cotton manufactory would undertake to maintain any of the children completely, and would satisfy the guardians that such children would be placed under proper care'.[33] This statement asserts the ideology of *laissez-faire* which sought to maintain a free market in goods and in labour. Similar thinking was applied to the relief of poverty.

The objective of the 1834 Poor Law Amendment Act was that able-bodied paupers who applied for poor relief allowances would no longer be given outdoor maintenance relief but, instead, recipients of state aid would have to enter the workhouse. What this legislation was attempting to do 'was the gradual substitution of relief in kind, *i.e.*, in bread and other necessaries, for relief in money.'[34] As a consequence, only those 'who were genuinely in dire need would accept the workhouse rather than starvation.'[35]

In the early nineteenth century the poor and the old lived in constant fear of being sent to the workhouse. In 1835, the Assistant Poor Law Commissioner, Charles Mott, identified the workhouse on Pennywell Road, in the parish of St Philip and St Jacob, the locality in which the cotton works was situated, as being in a particularly wretched state:

> The state of the workhouse was filthy in the extreme, the appearance of inmates dirty and wretched. There was no classification whatever, men, women, and children being promiscuously huddled together.[36]

Workhouses were used as instruments of discipline:

> to let the labourer find that the parish is the hardest taskmaster and the worst paymaster he can find, and thus induce him to make his application to the parish his last and not his first resource.[37]

33 Edwin Chadwick to the Clerk of the Guardians, Clifton Union, Bristol, published in the *Bristol Mercury*, 13 July 1839, p. 3.
34 Annual Report of the Poor Law Commissioners, Vol. 1 (London: HMSO, 1835), p. 7.
35 M. E. Rose, The Relief of Poverty 1834-1914 (London: Macmillan, 1972), p. 8.
36 Annual Report of the Poor Law Commissioners, Vol. 1 (London: HMSO, 1835), pp. 177-78.
37 Prepared by: Senior, Nassau. *Poor Law Commissioners' Report of 1834.* London: H.M. Stationery Office. 1905. Library of Economics and Liberty [Online] available from http://www.econlib.org/library/YPDBooks/Reports/rptPLC11.html; accessed 14 June 2015, Part II, Section 1.12.

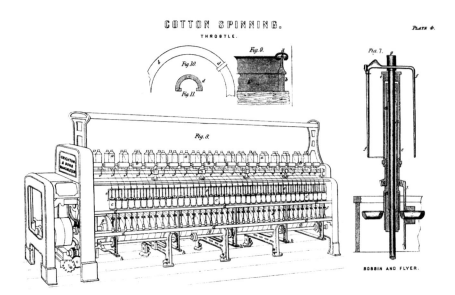

A throstle spinner.

No longer could the unemployed expect to draw outdoor relief. Therefore, as it was designed to do, the passing of the 1834 Poor Law Amendment Act raised the fear of the jobless having to enter the workhouse, which resulted in an increase in the pool of surplus labour competing for work. Nationally 'the number of paupers on [outdoor] relief fell from an estimated 1·26 million, 8·8 per cent of the population in 1834, to 1 million, 5·7 per cent of the population, in 1850.'[38]

Eager to find work, men, women and children, living both inside and outside the boundaries of the city of Bristol, provided an abundant supply of labour on which the new cotton works could draw. By 20 April 1840 the number of persons employed at the factory totalled 923, comprising 609 girls and 115 boys, aged between 13 and 14, 17 women, and 184 men.[39] Throstle spinning and weaving were occupations dominated by girls under the age of eighteen. Skilled men were brought in from Lancashire to run the self-acting (automatic) mule spinning machines bringing their families with them. They became influential in the development of the local community bringing with

---

38 Rose, *The Relief of Poverty 1834-1914*, p. 15.
39 These figures are taken directly from a loose insert in the Great Western Cotton Factory 'Dissected accounts' book, 9 October 1844 - 2 July 1845, Bristol Record Office; Also see Jones, 'The Cotton Industry in Bristol', These data differ from those published in *Bristol Mercury*, 2 May 1840, p. 2 and reproduced in a pamphlet by G. Atterton, *Cotton Threads: The History of the Great Western Cotton Factory* (Bristol: Barton Hill History Group, June 2015), p. 7.

Workers leaving the Great Western Cotton Works.

them some of their traditional ways such as clog dancing. They also imported long-standing habits of self-organization.

On arriving in Bristol they established a friendly society, the Great Western Oddfellowship Lodge.[40] This male only organization expected candidates for membership to be steady, respectable and reputable.[41] Approximately forty per cent of the men (seventy-four) employed at the cotton works were mechanics and foundry workers, and in 1839 they too set up an Oddfellowship Lodge called the Friendly Mechanics.[42] The lower paid who formed the vast majority of the workforce - 105 boys, 595 girls, and 12 women - were recruited mainly from the territory outside the city boundary stretching five miles east covering the districts of St. Jude, St. Philip and St. Jacob, Barton Hill, St. George, Hanham and Kingswood. They earned less than 7s per week; some of them took home as little as 1s per week (see table 1 below). Many households were dependent on both women's and children's earnings to supplement the family wage. As well as low wages short-term unemployment had a devastating affect on the lives of the people. Distinctions between the workforce were thus both gendered and based on geographical localities.

In 1838 the mill owners, some of them former slave-owners, drew glowing plaudits from the City's elites such as its Mayor, John Kerle Haberfield, fellow

40 *Western Daily Press*, 4 January 1938, p. 5.
41 See G. Crossick, 'The Labour Aristocracy and its Values: A Study of Mid-Victorian Kentish London', Victorian Studies, Vol. 19 No. 3 (March 1976), pp. 301-328.
42 *Western Daily Press*, 4 January 1938, p. 5.

Table 1 Wage Rates by age and gender, as at 20 April 1840

Rate per week	Girls (under 18)	Boys (under 18)	Women	Men	Total
1/-	4	9	0	0	13
1/6	58	4	0	0	62
1/8	44	0	0	0	44
2/-	13	12	0	0	25
2/6	8	6	0	0	14
3/-	19	13	0	0	32
3/4	50	0	0	0	50
3/6	120	12	0	0	132
4/-	21	19	1	0	41
4/6	14	14	0	0	28
5/-	117	9	3	0	129
5/6	15	1	1	0	17
6/-	11	6	0	0	17
6/6	20	0	0	0	20
6/8	81	0	7	0	88
7/-	12	0	3	4	19
8/-	0	0	0	2	2
9/-	2	1	0	7	10
10/-	0	1	2	28	31
12/-	0	6	0	11	17
13/-	0	0	0	5	5
14/-	0	0	0	5	5
15/-	0	0	0	5	5
16/-	0	0	0	8	8
17/-	0	0	0	1	1
18/-	0	0	0	8	8
20/-	0	0	0	15	15
21/-	0	0	0	1	1
24/-	0	0	0	24	24
26/-	0	0	0	6	6
27/-	0	0	0	9	9
28/-	0	0	0	16	16
30/-	0	0	0	8	8

Rate per week	Girls (under 18)	Boys (under 18)	Women	Men	Total
32/-	0	0	0	8	8
33/-	0	0	0	6	6
34/-	0	0	0	1	1
35/-	0	0	0	1	1
45/-	0	0	0	1	1
52/-	0	0	0	2	2
54/-	0	0	0	1	1
55/-	0	0	0	1	1
Total	**609**	**113**	**17**	**184**	**923**

Source: A loose insert, dated 20 April 1840, in the Great Western Cotton Factory 'Dissected accounts' book, 9 October 1844 - 2 July 1845, Bristol Record Office.

Town councillors, and members of the Bristol Chamber of Commerce, for bringing cotton manufacture to Bristol.[43] The untold reality of low wages, long hours, in dangerous and unhealthy conditions for the majority of workers was not revealed. Nor was the pressure of being subject to the ubiquitous authority of the cotton works' management and the dictates of the technological process. Work had to be done according to the pace of a machine 'under the close eye of overseers, enforcing assiduity by moral, pecuniary, occasionally even physical means of compulsion.'[44] In Frederick Engels' words cotton hands 'must eat, drink and sleep at command…The despotic bell calls him (*sic*) from his (*sic*) bed, his (*sic*) breakfast and his (*sic*) dinner.'[45]

43 *Bristol Mercury*, 21 April 1838, p. 4; *Bristol Mercury*, 18 May 1839, p. 3.
44 D. S. Landes, *The Unbound Prometheus: Technological Change and Industrial Development in Western Europe from 1750 to the Present* (Cambridge: Cambridge University Press, 1987, first published 1969), p. 43.
45 Engels, *The Condition of the Working Class in England*, p.467.

Chapter 2

Workers' Protests and the Courts

That all was not well in the factory came to light less than a year after the mill's opening when, in early February 1839, several workmen were dismissed for resisting certain rules and regulations. Their complaints had been:

1st, They were stopped half an hour for losing half a minute; 2nd, For losing half an hour they were suspended for the whole day; and 3rd, That an exorbitant charge was made for panes of glass accidentally or otherwise broke. To these rules they said they would never submit.[46]

Their case became public at a time of heightened protest against economic hardship and dreadful social conditions, often expressed through people's participation in Chartist processions which were held weekly in Bristol and finished with a rally on Brandon Hill. At one such parade, convened on the evening of February 1, 1839, Henry Vincent, a Chartist leader, led a procession on a white horse 'up Temple –street, over the bridge, up Bridge-street, Wine-street, past the Exchange, over the draw-bridge, through a portion of Clifton, and on to Brandon Hill' where around ten thousand people gathered to hear the speeches.[47]

Bristol's political establishment responded in differing ways. The *Bristol Mercury*, closely associated with the politics of Liberalism, chose not to send its correspondents to cover the meeting, ostensibly believing observations of its staff, from their publishing office in Broad Street, that the number of marchers present 'did not exceed 150',[48] grossly underestimating its enormity which was in the thousands. Similar processions and gatherings of comparable size (between five and ten thousand) ensued on the Thursday and Friday of the following week, just days before the dismissal of the dozen or so workers from the Great Western Cotton Works.

Instead of downplaying the support for Vincent's march the Tory Bristol newspaper, *Felix Farley's Journal*, dilated upon the size of the Bristol parades and the emotions of the crowds whipped up by the incendiary language deployed by the Chartist leaders. It opined:

46 *Bristol Mercury*, 16 February 1839, p. 3.
47 *The Charter*, 3 February 1839, p. 23; John Cannon mistakenly refers this claim by The Charter, of ten thousand attendees, to the meeting held on 31 January: J. Cannon, *The Chartists in Bristol* (Bristol: Bristol Branch of the Historical Association, 1964) p. 4.
48 *Bristol Mercury*, 2 February 1839, p. 3.

[W]e cannot refrain from directing the attention of our Magistrates to the danger that must arise if such meetings are allowed to be held every week. Letters from our correspondents describe the alarm they felt, as similar to that of the commencement of the [Bristol] Riots of 1831. A burnt child no doubt dreads the fire.[49]

Indeed, a little later, in early June 1839, two Chartists in Bristol were arrested and charged with possession of firearms, nine pistols and three powder flasks.[50]

Chartism had arisen partly in response to the upsurge in resistance to the new poor law causing considerable alarm to the ruling elite both nationally and locally.[51] Cotton factory operatives were among its most active supporters.[52] Whether a fear of wider social unrest influenced the decision of the owners of the Barton Hill cotton mill to step down and reemploy their dissident workers is impossible to determine. The official reason given for the settlement of the dispute was that it was based on a 'misunderstanding' in respect to the interpretation of the company rules and regulations.[53] However, such a reversal was uncommon and risked weakening managerial authority by undermining the decision to lay them off in in the first place.

By 1843, Bristolian fervour for, and faith in, Chartism had died down. However, workers' living conditions continued to be deplorable and in the parish of St. Philip and St. Jacob 'distress prevail[ed] to a lamentable extent'.[54] The factory had attracted an inflow of people 'in a locality where poverty and neglect were fast sinking a dense population in vice and misery.'[55] There was concern in middle-class circles that if unchecked this could lead to another era of contempt for authority, immorality and violent crime, raising the fear that in the event of a resurgence of Chartism the 'dangerous classes' (criminals, prostitutes and Juvenile delinquents) and the working classes could band together.[56]

49 *Felix Farley's Journal*, 3 February 1839.
50 *Taunton Courier & Western Advertiser*, 5 June 1839, p. 3.
51 *Bristol Mercury*, 25 May 1839, p. 3; See also Rose The Relief of Poverty 1834-1914, p. 10; and J. Knott, *Popular Opposition to the 1834 Poor Law* (London: Croom Helm, 1986).
52 D. Thompson, *The Chartists: Popular Politics in the Industrial Revolution* (Aldershot: Wildwood House, 1984), p. 107.
53 *Bristol Mercury*, 16 February 1839, p. 3.
54 *Bristol Mirror*, 1 January 1842, p. 5.
55 *Bristol Mercury*, 23 September 1843, p. 7.
56 For an examination of Victorian middle-class fears of an insurrectionary alliance between the dangerous classes and the labouring classes See V. Bailey, 'The Fabrication of Deviance: Dangerous Classes' and Criminal Classes' in Victorian Britain' in J. Rule and R. Malcolmson (eds.), *Protest and Survival: The Historical Experience, Essays for E. P. Thompson* (London: Merlin, 1993), Chapter Seven, pp. 221-257.

In their consideration of this problem, prevalent in many newly industrialized urban areas, the Government's response was to improve the education of children working in textile factories by drumming 'the right doctrines into people.'[57] Reform of standards was certainly required. The 1833 Factory Act had, not infrequently, allowed certificates of school attendance to be 'signed by the schoolmaster or schoolmistress with a cross, as they themselves were unable to write.'[58] The matter of education had been left to voluntary bodies, principally the Church. The largely non-conformist British and Foreign Schools Society and the Anglican National Society shared the small Government grant available.[59] In St. Philip's and Barton Hill the local children received their education from the Dings' Infant School, and later the Dings' British School, which was founded by non-conformists linked to the local Kingsland Chapel.[60] However, reformers' calls highlighting the need 'to withdraw child labour from the factories so that children might have time for education'[61] were ignored.

After 1838 the Dings' British School attended to the educational and spiritual development of many of the children employed at the Great Western Cotton Works. Anglicans, however, determined to seize the initiative away from non-conformists quickly sought to predominate in the instruction of local children, including those working at the cotton factory. On 24 May 1843, P.W.S. Miles laid the foundation stone for a new Anglican church located around 150 metres north of the factory in Church Street, just off Queen Ann Road. The Great Western Cotton Company contributed £1,000, Charles Pinney, £500 and Peter Aiken, £700, towards the £2,700 cost of building the church including, within its walls, a school.[62]

The Church of St. Luke was consecrated on 20 September 1843 by the Bishop of Bristol to provide moral and spiritual instruction to their workers, families and neighbours as a palliative for destitution and despair. The *Bristol Mercury* reported in delight 'that, in this neighbourhood at least, one large company [Great Western Cotton Mill] has not been unmindful of its responsibilities.'[63] As a key part of this project use was made of the crypt to provide up to 700 children with elementary education.[64]

57 B. Simon, *Studies in the History of Education, 1780-1870* (London:Lawrence & Wishart, 1960), p.165.
58 Karl Marx, *Capital* Volume 1 (London: New Left Review in association with Penguin Books, 1982, first edition published 1976), p. 523.
59 Simon, *Studies in the History of Education, 1780-1870*, p. 174.
60 *Bristol Mercury*, 23 July 1842, p. 8.
61 Simon, *Studies in the History of Education, 1780-1870*, p. 272.
62 Atterton, *Cotton Threads: The History of the Great Western Cotton Factory*, p. 16.
63 *Bristol Mercury*, 23 September 1843, p. 7.
64 *Bristol Times and Mirror*, 23 September 1843, p. 2..

In parallel with this development, the demand for places at the Dings' British School increased. By 1843 the school was full to capacity. The tobacco manufacturers, and Congregationalists, William D., Henry O. and Frederick Wills, and H. W. Benison, stepped in to supply most of the finance for the building of a new chapel and schoolhouse about 100 metres east of the cotton factory in Barton Street. The foundation stone was laid in June 1843.[65]

These developments coincided with vociferous debate over Sir James Graham's Factory Education Bill which was 'partly planned as a legislative antidote to the conditions which had helped to provoke the 'Plug Riots' of 1842'.[66] A series of strikes in the industrial districts became known as the Plug Plot after striking workers in industrial districts pulled the plugs out of steam engines in order to stop production. Riots ensued drawing a response from Graham in a speech he made in the House of Commons in March 1843.

I am informed, that the turbulent masses who, in the course of the last autumn, threatened the safety of property and disturbed the public peace in the manufacturing districts, were remarkable for the youth of the parties composing them... This circumstance shows the danger of neglecting the education of the rising generation.[67]

However, the educational clauses in Sir James Graham's Factory Bill of 1843 provoked an outcry especially from Non-conformists and Catholics. They were angered by the proposals that in effect gave preference to the Established Church as provider of education to children employed in textile companies. In Bristol, the Reverend Robert Thoresby, minister of the non-conformist Kingsland Chapel at St. Philip's, argued 'that the government had no right whatever to interfere with the education or the religion of the people.'[68] Dissenters feared that schools upheld and maintained by voluntary contribution would be destroyed.[69] Feared and hated, the Bill was vigorously opposed. The dissenters eventually triumphed. In the middle of June the Government conceded and withdrew all the education clauses from the Factory Bill.[70] The problem of children's education, however, remained.

65 *Bristol Mercury*, 10 June 1843, p. 6.
66 J. T. Ward and J. H. Treble 'Religion and Education in 1843: Reaction to the 'Factory Education Bill'', *The Journal of Ecclesiastical History*, Vol. 20, Issue 1, p. 79.
67 Sir James Graham's, Factories-Education: *Hansard*, 24 March 1843 Vol. 67 cc 1411-77.
68 *Bristol Times and Mirror*, 20 May 1843, p. 3.
69 Ward and Treble 'Religion and Education in 1843: Reaction to the 'Factory Education Bill'', p. 88.
70 Ward and Treble 'Religion and Education in 1843: Reaction to the 'Factory Education Bill'', p. 110.

Statistics available in 1841 revealed that out of around 31,200 children aged between five to fifteen years in the borough of Bristol, only 17,138 attended schools delivering some basic form of education. Therefore, apart from private or home instruction, 14,062 children for whatever reason did not attend any school.[71] Thus, after the withdrawal of the education clauses from the Factory Act, unsurprisingly there was a call to establish more non-sectarian schools to address the prevalence of 'vice and ignorance'. On 1 November 1843, a public meeting on this issue in Bristol, calling for the expansion of education on the principles of the British and Foreign School Society in the city, ended in disarray as the behaviour of some rowdy and unruly speakers proved too much for 'several of the more peaceful Dissenting ministers [who] left the platform and room.'[72]

For those in work, however, the harsh, regimented daily drudge of factory life overshadowed the hotly contested struggle between the Non-conformist and Anglican churches to provide their versions of the spiritual and educational needs of the Barton Hill people. Despite lacking formal organizational structures, workers adopted direct ways of protesting against the evils of factory work. On 9 October 1843 thirteen men and boys went absent from their employment at the cotton works without permission. They were brought before the Magistrates Court in front of Justices of the Peace and charged 'for having deserted their work.' [73] Having extracted a promise from the defendants that they would 'return to their duties' the company decided not 'to press the charge in the present instance…but they were determined on all future occasions to proceed to the utmost extremity of the law, which was the infliction of three months imprisonment.'[74]

The independence of the magistrates in this case was open to question as two of the three magistrates on the bench, Henry W. Newman and James George, were close associates of P. W. S. Miles, a partner in the Great Western Cotton Works. Newman and George had preceded Miles as Presidents of the Dolphin Society, a charity founded in 1749;[75] Miles was President in 1843.

71 *Bristol Times and Mirror*, 4 November 1843, p. 3.
72 *Bristol Times and Mirror*, 4 November 1843, p. 3.
73 Magistrates appointed to hear cases involving employment legislation were selected on the basis that they could not be a 'Proprietor or Occupier of or otherwise interested in' the mill or factory in question, or be related to the Proprietor or Occupier or interested person. See the 1833 (48) 3 Will. IV. -Sess. 1833, a bill to regulate the labour of children and young persons in the mills and factories of the United Kingdom, Clause 18, p. 6, (House of Commons Parliamentary Papers online).
74 *Bristol Times and Mirror*, 14 October 1843, p. 2.
75 Members of the Colston Society founded the Dolphin Society in 1749. On the 13 November every year, they commemorated the birthday of Edward Colston (1636-1721), a wealthy Bristol merchant who made his money from the slave trade.

Moreover, George was a former Mayor of Bristol and like Miles an active member of the Conservative Party.

On Thursday 9 November the company was in Court again. This time, however, it was to answer a charge of not giving due notice to two girls they had dismissed from their employment at the mill. As the girls could not provide a written contract saying they were entitled to receive two weeks notice, the case was dismissed.[76] The Court, however, could not discount two other charges brought against Joseph Clarke, the leading partner in the Great Western Cotton Works.

At the same 9 November Court sessions Clarke appeared before the local magistrates summoned for offences against the Factory Act. Representing himself and his co-partners in the company he faced the charge of working all the young persons under eighteen years of age employed at the mill for more than twelve hours a day. He pleaded guilty. He was convicted and ordered to pay a penalty of £10, and costs of 5s. The Court directed that the penalty be paid to Hannah Moore's School, in the parish of St. Philip and Jacob.[77]

This was not the first time that Clarke had shown indifference to children's welfare. In the early 1830s he had owned or managed Holt Town Mills, Manchester. In 1832-3 he had provided written responses to the Central Board of His Majesty's commissioners, appointed to collect information in the manufacturing districts, as to the employment of children in factories and as to the propriety and means of curtailing the hours of their labour.

This survey took place before the outset of the 1834 Factories Inquiry Commission and prior to the passing of the 1833 Factory Act. In a written answer to a query raised as to whether arrangements for health or convenience of his workpeople were available in his factory, he entered 'none'. And in response to the question 'what is the lowest age at which you employ children', he wrote 'from seven upwards: this business not being regulated by Act of Parliament'.[78] He had no such excuse to fall back on in 1843. His continued indifference to children's health and welfare in the workplace reflected the attitude of many mill owners in this period making a mockery of the bland retrospective assertions that the proprietors of the Great Western Cotton Works showed 'concern for

76 *Bristol Mercury*, 11 November 1843, p. 4.
77 Factories Acts: A return of the number and names of persons summoned for offences against the Factories Act, between 1 January 1843 and 1 January 1844, HOUSE OF COMMONS PAPERS; ACCOUNTS AND PAPERS, Paper No.106, Vol. XXXIX, P. 275, (House of Commons Parliamentary Papers online); *Bristol Mercury*, 11 November 1843, p. 4.
78 1834 (167) Factories Inquiry Commission. Supplementary report of the Central Board of His Majesty's commissioners appointed to collect information in the manufacturing districts, as to the employment of children in factories, and as to the propriety and means of curtailing the hours of their labour. Part 1, p. 179 (House of Commons Parliamentary Papers online).

the welfare of their workers'.[79] The actual scenario can be read through the long catalogue of legal cases and reports of accidents, as well as instances of labour rebellion.

On the 1 December for the second time the company was brought before the local Magistrates Court, this time on two charges. The first one concerned meal break allowances. The company was found guilty of not giving their young employees their full entitlement of one and a half hours for meals, as stipulated in the Factory Act. This time the Court imposed a penalty of £20 to be paid to Hannah Moore's School, Trinity Road, St. Philip's, a school founded in 1838 'for the education of the poor in the principles of the established church'.[80]

The second charge was more serious. The Factory Act determined that every mill register the starting and finishing times of its employees, including meal breaks, in a 'Time Book'. Companies found to make false entries in the 'Book' could expect to receive a fine of between £50 and £100.[81] Appearing for the company, Clarke, although having had announced his retirement as a partner at the end of August 1843,[82] pleaded guilty to 'entering in the Register of Time lost, on 20th and 21st November, a greater number of hours than were actually lost' by his workers on those days. The company got off lightly, however, with a £20 fine plus costs of 9s 6d for each offence. Hannah More's and the British and Foreign Schools were beneficiaries of the fines.[83] In this case the magistrate, James Evans Lunell, was a Liberal councillor and the Chairman of the British and Foreign School Society, which explains why this school was included to be one of the recipients of the financial penalty imposed on the company. Formed in 1808 the British and Foreign School Society drew its inspiration from the work of the Quaker educationalist, Joseph Lancaster.[84]

79 For example see Jennings, *Societies in the Making*, p. 22.

80 *Bristol Mercury*, 15 September 1838, p. 3.

81 1833 (48) 3 Will. IV. -Sess. 1833. A bill to regulate the labour of children and young persons in the mills and factories of the United Kingdom, Clause 25, p. 9.

82 See the Partnership Deeds concerning the arrangement on the retirement of J. B. Clarke from the Great Western Cotton Works, Bristol Record Office. This announcement did not stop him from continuing to work for the Company.

83 Factories Acts: A return of the number and names of persons summoned for offences against the Factories Act, between 1 January 1843 and 1 January 1844, p. 275; *Bristol Mercury*, 2 December 1843, p. 8.

84 *Bristol Mercury*, 12 June 1841, p. 8.

Chapter 3

A Dangerous Place to Work: Workplace Accidents

These displays of company arrogance and flippancy towards the law and the welfare of its employees, so soon after the opening of the factory, were not untypical of cotton manufacturers. However, from outside the industry calls for reform, particularly from a conservative critique of the consequences of liberal *laissez-faire*, were being made nationally. Social and political radicals agitated for regulation from a moral humanitarian consideration with well-being and a fear that the factory system would give rise to social disintegration. Women and children in the weavers' sheds endured a hot, damp and muggy atmosphere every working day.[85] Dust in the card room was another hazard. An agitator for factory reform, Charles Turner Thackrah, a Leeds surgeon, asserted that 'adults, who have been long in the [Cotton] employ, not infrequently suffer from affection of the lungs', although workers rarely complained.[86]

Another health issue, unheeded for many years, was the spread of disease caused by the system of 'kissing the shuttle', which involved weavers replenishing empty shuttles. This process entailed drawing the cotton thread through the shuttle's eyelet hole using mouth suction. As a consequence of this action, which was carried out hundreds of times per day, weavers regularly inhaled dirt, fine lint and other potentially health threatening substances. In Britain it was well into the twentieth century before shuttle kissing was officially recognized as dangerous to health.[87]

Even more palpable, however, and attracting greater public attention, were the high accident rates among factory workers which were often associated with the intensification of work and the piece-rate structure of pay. In the cotton industry this pay system habitually enticed some workers to risk cleaning machinery in motion, which occasionally resulted in disablement and, sometimes, premature death. Self-righteous employers were inclined to blame the high accident rates on workers for not taking due care and attention. This obviated employers from taking any responsibility for injuries sustained by

85 Engels, The Condition of the Working Class in England, p. 443.

86 C. Turner Thackrah, *The Effects of the principal Arts, Trades, and Professions, and of civic states and habits of living on Health and Longevity* (London: Longman, Rees, Orme, Brown, & Green, 1831), p. 74.

87 J. Greenlees, "Stop Kissing and Steaming!': Tuberculosis and the occupational health movement in Massachusetts and Lancashire, 1870-1918', *Urban History*, Vol. 32:2, August 2005, pp227-233: P. Dale, J. Greenlees and J. Melling, 'The Kiss of Death or a Flight of Fancy? Workers' health and the campaign to regulate shuttle kissing in the British cotton industry, c. 1900-52, *Social History*, Vol. 32:1, February 2007, pp. 54-75.

their employees and left underlying causes unaddressed. Consequently, in 1833 the Factory Commissioners attempted to make textile employers vicariously liable for the actions of their employees. They proposed

> that in the case of all accidents whatsoever from machinery occurring to children under fourteen years of age, the proprietor of the machinery shall pay for the medical attendance on the child, and all the expenses of the cure, until medical attendance is no longer required; and also during the same period shall continue to pay wages at the rate of half the wages enjoyed by the individual in question at the time of the occurrence of the accident.[88]

Despite this pronouncement the problem of industrial accident liability remained unclear.[89] Ostensibly, the civil action case of Priestley v Fowler in 1837 established 'the principle that an employer owed a common law duty of care which was actionable if a breach of that duty resulted in injury.'[90] It was not until the powers incorporated into the 1844 Factory Amendment Act that factory inspectors could order factory owners to fence what they considered as dangerous machinery and could bring an action to recover damages on behalf of any person injured by machinery, though this did not extend to those fatally injured.[91] In August 1846 the Fatal Accidents Compensation Act became law which provided the dependents of the deceased the right to compensation, but any such claim had to be 'brought about by the executor or administrator of the deceased', and not by the factory inspector or a coroner. In such cases the jury could award damages 'proportioned to the injury resulting from such death'.[92]

However, 'the wording of the fencing clauses' of the 1844 Factory Amendment Act was left 'wide open to magistrate interpretation.'[93] Even with

88 *Report of the Commissioners on Conditions in Factories* (House of Commons Parliamentary Papers online), 1833, XX, pp. 68-75.
89 P. Kirby, *Child Workers and Industrial Health in Britain, 1780-1850* (Woodbridge, Suffolk: Boydell Press, 2013), p. 97.
90 D. Eves, 'Two steps forward, one step back' A brief history of the origins, development and implementation of health and safety law in the United Kingdom, 1802-2014. http://www.historyofosh.org.uk/brief/ accessed 25/12/2015.
91 *The Times*, 'The Factory Act', 1 October 1844, p. 6.
92 1846 (560) Death by accidents compensation. A bill [as amended by the Select Committee] intituled, an act for compensating the families of persons killed by accidents, (House of Commons Parliamentary Papers online), Act passed in August 1846.
93 P. Bolin-Hort, 'Government Inspectors and the Regulation of Industry: On the Problem of True Enforcement of the Early British Factory Acts' in *Bringing in the Inspector: the Framing and Enforcement of the Early Factory Legislation in Britain, 1825-1900*, Working Papers on Childhood and the Study of Children (Stockholm: Department of Child Studies, Linköping University, 1996), p. 49.

the power given to factory inspectors to bring actions against mill owners in the case of accidents stemming from insecurely fenced machinery, reported accidents in the cotton industry increased over the following year. In the half-year ending 30 April 1845 the weekly average of reported accidents was thirty-three; in the half-year ending 31 October 1845 they were forty-five weekly; and in the half-year ending 30 April 1846 they averaged more than forty-seven weekly.[94] It was 1847 before the rate of accidents in the industry began to fall.

On 5 July 1845, the *Bristol Times and Mirror* published a letter, signed 'Z', highlighting the frequency of accidents at the renamed Great Western Cotton Works, Maze, Ames, Bush & Company, presenting some examples that had occurred in the first half of 1845. It was an extremely polite letter that went out of its way not to place blame on the mill's proprietors, whose 'high character... active benevolence, and practical philanthropy', the writer said, was not in doubt. The correspondent's objective was to bring public attention to the high accident rate at the cotton works in order 'to prevent if possible their so frequent recurrence.'[95] The actual accidents disclose the terrible consequences behind the drive for profit providing the wealth that made benevolent philanthropy possible. The polite correspondent was in fact drawing attention to the repeated assaults upon the bodies of the poor.

Table 2 below summarizes **reported** accidents published in local newspapers between the construction of the mill in 1837 and February 1847.

Table 2 reveals that during this period many of the injuries suffered by children at the Great Western Cotton Works had been as a result of them becoming entangled in machinery. Z's letter to the editor of the *Bristol Times and Mirror* drew attention to the 1844 Factory Amendment Act:

> Section 20 enacts, - "That no child or young person shall be allowed to clean any part of the mill-gearing in a factory, while in motion; or to work between the fixed and traversing part of any self-acting machine while the latter is in motion by the action of the steam—engine, water wheel, or other mechanical power.[96]

Here the author is questioning why so many children and young people had become caught in moving machinery. He went on to quote sections 21-25

94 1846 (721) Reports of the inspectors of factories to Her Majesty's Principal Secretary of State for the Home Department, for the half-year ending 30th April, 1846, (House of Commons Parliamentary Papers online); 1847 (828) Reports of the inspectors of factories to Her Majesty's Principal Secretary of State for the Home Department, for the half-year ending 30th April, 1847, (House of Commons Parliamentary Papers online).
95 *Bristol Times & Mirror*, 5 July 1845, p. 4.
96 *Bristol Times & Mirror*, 5 July 1845, p. 4

Table 2 Accounts of accidents at the Great Western Cotton Works, published in local newspapers between January 1839 and February 1847.

Year & Month	Cause of Accident	Injuries/fatalities	Source
1839 (Jan)	Two labourers crushed by a 50cwt large wheel while unloading heavy machinery	Both died	*Taunton Courier & Western Advertiser*, 23 Jan. 1839
1842 (Apr)	Caroline Pike, aged 15, reprimanded and physically assaulted by an overlooker	Suffered an epileptic fit and died, Verdict Died of epilepsy	*Bristol Times & Mirror*, 30 April 1842
1842 (Jul)	John Stubbings, 20 years of age, tripped over the ledge of a scaffold	Fell to his death, Verdict Accidental death	*Bristol Times & Mirror*, 9 July 1842
1842 (Mar)	Mary Ann Adams, aged 17, caught the sleeve of her gown in a machine	Badly Lacerated	*Bristol Times & Mirror*, 26 March 1842
1842 (Apr)	Rhoda Green, aged 13, caught her hand in machinery.	One finger torn off	*Bristol Mercury*, 16 April 1842
1842 (Oct)	Richard Hall, aged 14, right hand got caught in some machinery	Lost a thumb and two fingers	*Bristol Mirror*, 15 October 1842, p. 8.
1842 (Oct)	George Alexander, a weaver aged 46. While cleaning his machine he caught his thumb in one of the wheels	Thumb torn off	*Bristol Mercury*, 5 November 1842
1843 (Jan)	John Huxtable, aged 25, caught his arm in machinery	Arm amputated	*Bristol Mercury*, 21 Jan. 1843
1844 (Jul)	Thomas Farley, aged 14, machine wheel ran over his middle finger, crushing it in the process	Died, constitution irritation, Verdict: Accidental death	*Bristol Mercury*, 6 July 1844
1844 (Jul)	Michael Jones, a boy, caught his hand in machinery	Severely lacerated	*Bristol Times & Mirror*, 6 July 1844
1844 (Jul)	James Wilson, a carpenter, aged 28, unknown how injury was sustained	Severely lacerated	*Bristol Times & Mirror*, 6 July 1844

Year & Month	Cause of Accident	Injuries/fatalities	Source
1844 (Jul)	Benjamin Canes, a boy, caught his thigh in machinery	Dreadfully lacerated	*Bristol Times & Mirror*, 13 July 1844
1844 (Oct)	Jones (possibly the same boy injured in July) caught his arm in machinery	Severely lacerated	*Bristol Times & Mirror*, 19 October 1844
1844 (Nov)	Louisa Stokes, aged 25, caught her hand in machinery	Lost one finger and the rest of the hand severely lacerated	*Bristol Times & Mirror*, 30 Nov. 1844
1844 (Dec)	Joseph Grimes, a boy, aged 15, fell thirty feet	Sustained severe injuries	*Bristol Times & Mirror*, 21 Dec. 1844
1845 (Jan)	Chamberlain, a young women, caught her hand in machinery	One finger cut off and severely lacerated hand	*Bristol Times & Mirror*, 18 Jan. 1845
1845 (Jan)	Langstreeth, a young girl – a trap door fell on her head	Fractured Skull	*Bristol Times & Mirror*, 18 Jan. 1845
1845 (Jan)	William Bryant, aged 14, fell from the fourth story to the ground	Severely injured	*Bristol Times & Mirror*, 1 Feb. 1845
1845 (Jan)	Two boys, John Dillon , aged 16, and William Kerby, aged 15, hands caught in machinery	Severely injured	*Bristol Times & Mirror*, 1 Feb. 1845
1845 (Apr)	Isaac Biddle, hand caught in machinery	Hand severely lacerated	*Bristol Times & Mirror*, 5 July. 1845
1845 (Apr)	Abraham Bridle, aged 19, hand caught in machinery	Hand severely lacerated	*Bristol Times & Mirror*, 5 July. 1845
1845 (May)	William Blannin, aged 14, arm caught in machinery	Arm severely lacerated	*Bristol Times & Mirror*, 5 July. 1845
1845 (Jun 1845)	Emma Ward, aged 22, tangled her hand and arm in machinery	Lost middle finger and two tendons ten inches in length attached to it	*Bristol Times & Mirror*, 5 July. 1845
1845 (Oct)	Henry Clargo, aged 16, caught in machinery	Head severely lacerated	*Bristol Times & Mirror*, 18 Oct. 1845
1846 (Jan)	Iles, little boy, hand caught in machinery	One finger amputated	*Bristol Times & Mirror*, 17 Jan. 1846
1846 (Sept)	Adam Sheppard, aged 15, caught in machinery	Fractured arm and lacerations	*Bristol Times & Mirror*, 3 Oct. 1846
1847 (Feb)	Henry Bennett, aged 20, caught in a dash wheel driven by a steam engine	Died of his injuries	*Bristol Mercury*, 6 Feb. 1847

of the Act suggesting that managers of the local cotton works should ensure that they fully comply with the Act in future in order to reduce the number of accidents occurring at their factory.

The following week's edition of the *Bristol Times and Mirror*, 12 July 1845, published a notice saying that 'Z's' letter, containing a veiled critique of the safety record at Great Western Cotton Works, had subsequently been contended. The paper outlined the objection it had received which argued 'that, taking the large number constantly employed in the works, there are not so many accidents there as take place at any other factory of a like size (a statement which we believe is correct).' The paper went on to say that it felt the proprietors took every reasonable precaution to prevent accidents, thus no culpability could be attached to them.[97]

While accidents at the Great Western Cotton Works may have been no higher than elsewhere in England, this failure to acknowledge the link between the causation of accidents with the organization of work is an example of cotton proprietors' aloofness and detachment from the world of work experienced by their employees, despite reports from factory inspectors recommending that accident prevention could be enhanced 'by greater precaution in fencing off the more dangerous places.[98] The evidence presented in Table 2 suggests that the reason behind many of the accidents recorded at the Great Western Cotton Works was due to the lack of enforcement in fencing off moving machine parts.

However, injury or death at work continued to be regarded as contingent risk. In the cases of fatalities resulting from industrial accidents recorded in Table 2, it is particularly notable that the coroners' hearings resulted in verdicts of accidental death. This tells us something about the society and culture in which these accidents happened, and the failure of companies to take any meaningful action to prevent them or accept any responsibility when they occurred. The individual tragedy of a fourteen year-old orphan boy, Thomas Farley, is a particularly revealing case.

Adversity struck a fortnight after Farley, a recruit from the Stroud Union Workhouse, had started work at the Great Western Cotton Factory. In stooping to pick up cotton waste under self-acting mules in motion he caught one of his fingers in a machinery wheel. Immediately following his mishap he went to the infirmary, where he received only rudimentary treatment to his hand. He was sent home in great distress and spent the rest of the weekend in bed. On Monday morning he went to work despite suffering extreme pain in his

97 *Bristol Times & Mirror*, 12 July 1845, p. 3.
98 Report by R. J. Saunders, 1844 (583) Reports of the inspectors of factories to Her Majesty's Principal Secretary of State for the Home Department, for the half-year ending 30th June, 1844, (House of Commons Parliamentary Papers online).

Mule Spinning and Scavengers and piecers.

severely swollen middle finger, but after returning to his lodgings for breakfast he felt unable to return to the mill and resume his employment. His condition deteriorated. At one o'clock he was taken to see the Great Western Cotton Works' surgeon who changed the dressing but confidently diagnosed that there was no immediate danger, and no need to prescribe medication. After returning home, and feeling feverish, Farley went straight to bed. The next day he was found to be much worse and the works' assistant surgeon was called for. He prescribed some medicine to calm the fever which the boy took later at around six in the evening. The following morning he died. The cause of his death was later judged to be an extreme degree of 'constitutional irritation' and symptomatic fever.[99] However, the lack of urgency apparent in the response of both the Bristol Royal Infirmary and the works' surgeon are likely to have contributed to his death.

Public attention to tragedies such as this one, however, very gradually brought about a process where 'workplace accidents were ideologically reconstituted, from individual human tragedies into a social problem that could only be solved by government intervention'.[100] During the mid 1850s this interventionist shift met with strong resistance from some employers organized in the National Association of Factory Occupiers who lobbied against what they deemed as meddling legislation. Although there is no evidence to suggest the proprietors of Bristol's cotton works joined this organization, it will be seen later that where the company saw loopholes in the legislation it did its utmost to avoid paying out compensation to victims of industrial accidents.

99 This account is based on reports published in *Bristol Mercury*, 6 July 1844, p. 8 and *Bristol Times and Mirror*, 6 July 1844, p. 3.
100 J. Bronstein, Caught in the Machinery: Workplace Accidents and Injured Workers in Nineteenth-Century Britain, (California: Stanford University Press, 2007), p. 170.

Chapter 4

Pleasures and Perils

The creation of large factories like the Great Western Cotton Company brought into being a social and cultural world with on which new rituals emerged. Employers favoured forms that encouraged workers to identify themselves with the company, seeking to secure their loyalty. The paternalistic organization of leisure time complemented regular timekeeping and workplace discipline.[101] Such rituals of benevolence did not necessarily fool workers. For example, Patrick Joyce quotes one beneficiary of a works' dinner party in Ashton-under-Lyne as not being duped by such treats: 'Our masters think to put us off with a plate of beef and a glass of beer, but he will find himself mistaken. What we want is more wages, and we will have it before we have done.'[102]

The Great western Cotton Company's annual beano provided a brief respite from the hazardous and brutal workplace environment of the cotton factory and became established as a tradition. Weston-super-Mare, Clevedon and Bath were some of the popular destinations. In contrast to the largely unregulated, and sometimes unruly, social life of the workers at this time, these trips tended to be regimented affairs organized and controlled by the company, as evidenced by the organization, form and atmosphere of the June 1849 outing.

Numbering around 1,000, employees of the Great Western Cotton Company assembled outside the mill's gates at six o'clock on Saturday 2 June. On receiving their tickets they formed a procession and, accompanied by bands of music and carrying a variety of flags and banners, they proceeded to the railway station. The order of procession was telling. At the front, draped in a union jack, was a large horse drawn wagon carrying the Hanham music band followed by eight business associates of the company's proprietors on horseback. The main body of the procession was divided into nine sections representing the various production departments, each carrying its own banner and each section led by two overlookers on horseback. Craft workers, labourers and clerks were also represented. The winders and warpers carried a banner emblazoned with the words 'Success to the Proprietors of the Great Western Cotton Works' and

---

101 For a classic fictional account of the Beano see Robert Tressell, *The Ragged Trousered Philanthropists* (London: Lawrence and Wishart, 1985, first complete edition, 1955), Chapter 44; Also see E. P. Thompson 'Time, Work-Discipline and Industrial Capitalism' in E. P. Thompson, *Customs in Common* (London: Merlin, 1991), Chapter VI.
102 P. Joyce, *Work, Society & Politics: The Culture of the Factory in Later Victorian England* (London: Methuen, 1980), p. 149.

the card room hands toted a banner bearing the words 'Success to the City and trade of Bristol'.[103]

On arriving at their destination, Weston-super-Mare, the procession reformed and marched through the town before dispersing with a shilling each in their pockets given to them by their employer to enjoy the delights of the seaside for the rest of the day. They reassembled in the evening and marched back through the town to the railway station to catch the train home. However, the ordering of pleasure could not prevent the ravages of epidemics and the danger of fire. The annual works' Beano was a show of stability amidst most uncertain circumstances, not just economically but in the panics that surround disease and catastrophes.

A few weeks after the works' Beano event in Weston-super-Mare 'the first well-marked case of cholera in Bristol occurred in a boy resident in Chapel-court, St. James Back, who worked and was taken ill at the Cotton factory, and who died in a few hours.'[104] This outbreak of cholera in Bristol peaked in July, August and September 1849.[105] Death rates mounted notably in the poorer overcrowded industrial districts of inner and outer Bristol where there was the absence of an effective water supply and sewerage system; for example the parish of St. Luke's, Barton Hill, burials rose from nineteen in 1848 to thirty-one in 1849.[106] The most likely cause for this increase in the mortality rate was the cholera epidemic. Indeed, the Bristol physician, Dr. William Budd, subsequently noted in an article: 'in every former outbreak [of cholera]' St. Philip's had been badly affected. He added that it 'long had an evil notoriety as a very hot-bed of contagious disorders'.[107]

Budd accumulated a considerable body of knowledge about the disease through his work as a physician to the Bristol Royal Infirmary and from new observations laid before the Bristol Medico-Chirurgical Society.[108] In September 1849, Budd argued that contaminated drinking water was 'the chief vehicle of the poison'.[109] Only a month before the better known Dr. John Snow had come to the same conclusion. Unlike Snow, however, Budd continued to believe that cholera also could be transmitted through the air,

---

103 *Bristol Times and Mirror*, 9 June 1849, p. 5.
104 *Bristol Times and Mirror*, 30 June 1849, p. 8.
105 G. Munro Smith, 'Cholera Epidemics in Bristol in the Nineteenth Century', *The British Medical Journal*, 10 July 1915, p. 60.
106 W. Sanigar, *Leaves of a Barton Hill Notebook* (Bristol: University Settlement, 1954), p. 36.
107 W. Budd, 'Asiatic Cholera in Bristol in 1866', *British Medical Journal*, 13 April 1867, p. 413.
108 W. Budd, 'Malignant Cholera: its cause, mode of propagation, and prevention' reprinted in the *International Journal of Epidemiology*, 2013: 42: p. 1567. (First published in 1849, London: Churchill).
109 Budd, 'Malignant Cholera', p. 1571.

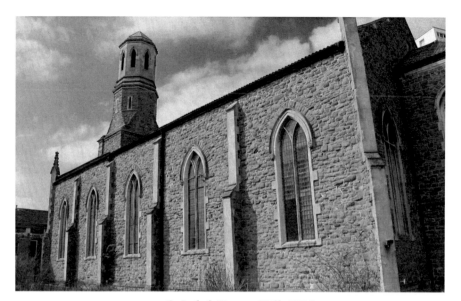

St Luke's Barton Hill, 2016.

St Lukes Barton Hill, 2016.
The junction of Queen Ann Road and Avondale Road.

not by the means of inhalation, as previously thought, but 'in the act of swallowing'.[110]

It took several years for the water based theory to be generally accepted but Budd took up the practical aspect of purifying water supplies by becoming one of the early directors of the Bristol Waterworks Company on the stipulation that the water supply 'should be drawn from sources beyond the possible reach of sewage contamination'.[111]

Bristol Waterworks Company had been established through an Act of Parliament in July 1846 to supply water to the whole city and not just the affluent area of Clifton. The magnitude of this task, however, meant that in 1849 it was still work-in-progress.[112] Moreover, it was cost conscious. It was only during the cholera epidemic that the company agreed to supply water 'without charge' to the Cholera Hospital in Peter Street on the proviso that the hospital would bare the cost of laying the service pipe from the main, and that the company 'retain the right of discontinuing the supply at their pleasure.'[113]

As the cholera crisis subsided, on Friday 12 October 1849 a serious fire broke out at the Great Western Cotton premises in Barton Hill. A spark from a flywheel ignited a pile of unprepared cotton in the blowing room causing extensive damage to the building and machinery. Fortunately, around 100 employees, predominately boys and girls, working in the building managed to escape without sustaining injury. The fire raged for hours and flames were visible across the city and at one point threatened to spread to the rest of the factory. It took several fire appliances to contain the fire. The damaged incurred (see Figure 1 below), estimated to be valued at around £15,000, was covered by insurance. The biggest losers were the 2,000 factory hands put out-of-work. They had to wait six long weeks before repairs were sufficiently advanced to enable the rehiring of many, but not all, of those who had been laid-off.[114]

In a letter to the editor of the *Bristol Mercury*, an unnamed employee of the cotton works praised John Ashworth, the thirty-two years old works' manager, for the relief he paid out to 'all the workpeople whom he considered in distress,

110 Budd, 'Malignant Cholera, p. 1570. For a more detailed and nuanced review of the work of Snow, Budd and other less celebrated nineteenth century studies about the cause of cholera see G. Davey Smith 'Commentary: Behind the Broad Street Pump: aetiology, epidemiology and prevention of cholera in mid-19th century Britain', *International Journal of Epidemiology*, 2002: 31: pp. 920-932.

111 J. Thornton and P. Pearson, 'Bristol Water Works Company; a study of nineteenth century resistance to local authority purchase attempts', *Water History*, 5 (3), 2013, p. 315.

112 *Bristol Mercury*, 'Bristol Water Works", 17 March 1849, p. 4.

113 *Bristol Times and Mirror*, 1 September 1849, p. 5.

114 *Bristol Mercury*, 20 October 1849, p. 3; John Bull (London), 20 October 1849, Issue 1, 506, p. 666.

Feeder Canal

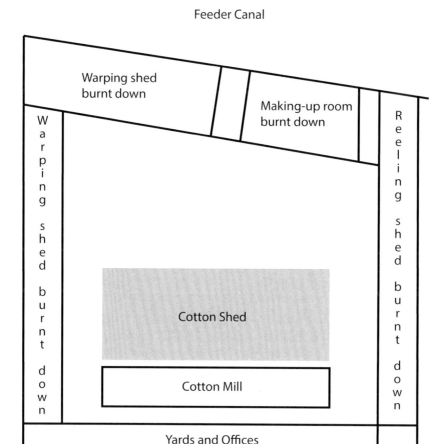

Figure 1: Sketch source Bristol Times and Mirror, 1 June 1850, p. 8.

during the five (*sic*) weeks the mill was stopped'. He finished his letter with the words 'no proprietors could do more for such a number of people (nearly 2000) than ours have done.'[115] Reverend C. G. Young, of Kingsland Chapel, St. Philip's, however, strongly challenged the veracity of this tribute. He contended that the relief distributed by Ashworth was totally inadequate, very few workers laid off because of the fire 'received more than 9d., and many only 6d. or 4d., while the great proportion had nothing whatever… a poor set-off against six weeks loss of work'.[116] He went on to say that many of the girls were taken back on short-time and it would be months before they could retrieve their clothes out of pawn.

Notably, Young's Kingsland Chapel attracted far greater congregations than St. Luke's Church which had owed its origin largely to the patronage of Great Western Cotton Factory. For instance, average attendance at St. Luke's, which could hold over 1,000 people, was less than 100 at its Sunday services, while Kingsland Chapel attracted around 400 worshipers.[117] Young had, along with tobacco industrialists W.D. and H.O Wills, raised £11 from a public appeal to help the laid-off cotton workers during their time of great distress, which was distributed among a hundred of the most needy.[118]Little did he know that within six months disaster would yet again befall the cotton works.

In the early hours of Thursday 30 May 1850 another fire struck the cotton works destroying the reeling and warping sheds and all the machinery and stock it contained. Consequently, once more 2,000 hands were thrown out of work. Apart from one firefighter who fractured a leg no one was hurt. The blaze started close to either the making- up room or in the corner of the warping shed under suspicious circumstances. It was 'strongly suspected to be the work of an incendiary.' Apart from two 'trusted' night watchmen no one was on the premises. It was summer and the gas lighting had not been used for several weeks. Nothing stored in the sheds was of a nature that could have caused spontaneous combustion. As in the previous fire the buildings were covered by insurance.[119]

A search of the local newspapers has not revealed how this fire was started. Nor is it stated when production at the cotton works resumed. However, it does reveal how the differentiations between workers had become internalized. Following the fire a speech at a social event (special invitation only) indicated

115 *Bristol Mercury*, 15 December 1849, p. 8.
116 *Bristol Mercury*, 22 December 1849, p. 3.
117 A. Munden (ed.), *Religious Census of Bristol & Gloucestershire 1851*, Vol. 29 (Bristol: The Bristol & Gloucestershire Archaeological Society, 2015), p. 81-82.
118 *Bristol Mercury*, 17 November 1849 p. 8, and 22 December 1849, p. 3.
119 *Bristol Times and Mirror* 1 June 1850, p. 8.

tension between Ashworth and certain sections of the workforce. In contrast he was on good terms with the highly skilled mechanics. On Saturday evening 3 August around fifty mechanics employed at the Great Western Cotton Works invited the works' manager, Ashworth, to a dinner at the Lamb Inn, West Street, Old Market. This occasion was especially arranged by the mechanics to give them the chance to thank Ashworth, who had been managing the works since 1844,[120] for his benevolence towards them:

> We rejoice at having this opportunity of expressing our gratitude to you for the interest you have always manifested in our welfare, especially at a time when others have been through unforeseen calamities deprived of that employment which afforded them the means of existence. It affords us much pleasure to find that the malicious aspersions and base insinuations, endeavoured to be hurled at your character by a few cowardly miscreants, have not in the least degree affected the regard we one and all feel towards you.[121]

The mechanics had played a key role in repairing the damage and destruction caused by two major fires that had occurred at the cotton works within a very short period of time. Unsurprisingly, therefore, Ashworth acted favourably towards them, as their cooperation was essential in getting the cotton works back in production. This accentuated the cultural division that already existed between craft (all men) and non-craft workers. This skill and gender differentiation was visibly reflected in how the mechanics dressed outside the workplace. At their Lodge meetings, and other social occasions, the mechanics sported top hats and frock coats.[122] The social gulf between this new kind of skilled working class 'aristocrat' and the rest continued to be marked well into the twentieth century.

120 *Bristol Times and Mirror*, 15 December 1849, p. 8.
121 *Bristol Times and Mirror*, 10 August 1850, p. 5.
122 *Western Daily Press*, 4 January 1938, p. 5.

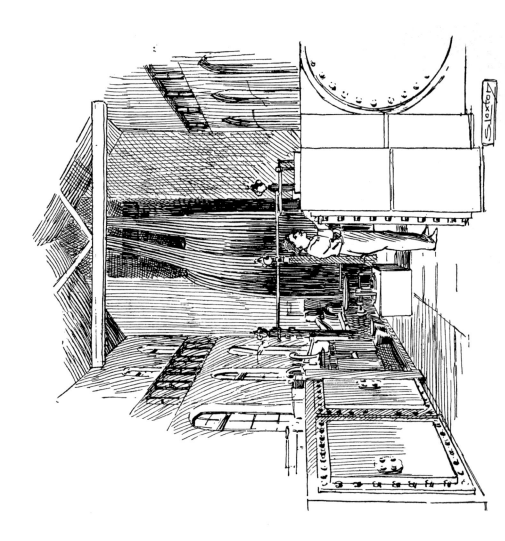

Part 2 The Mid-Century

Chapter 5

Resistance and Riots

By the mid-October 1850 the Great Western Cotton Company was back on its feet with plans to meet increased demand by procuring additional machinery for the weaving department.[123] This expansion required more labour. Ashworth, in his hunt for new recruits, turned to Belfast where the cotton industry had long been in decline.[124] He brought over several girls giving them hope of steady employment and a new life. However, in the New Year orders dried up and some of the Belfast girls were laid off. Destitute and extremely distressed one of them, Ann Murphy, stole a shawl and pawned it.

On Saturday 15 February she was brought before the local magistrates who were informed of the circumstances of her detention. On learning that Ashworth had brought Murphy along with some other girls from Belfast to Bristol to work at the Great Western Cotton Works, the Conservative Mayor and Chief Magistrate, John Kerle Haberfield, remarked 'if that is so, it is cruel conduct not to take care of them.' Haberfield's response demonstrates a view of employers' protective obligation to young women workers and Murphy was discharged on the promise that she would return the shawl to its rightful owner. Clearly disturbed by Murphy's plight, Haberfield, who was also a governor of the Bristol Corporation of the Poor, ordered that the prisoner be given 2s from the poor box.[125]

Ashworth was furious. He contacted Police Inspector Webb who was in charge of the case and informed him that Murphy had left her employment voluntarily and had since absconded with some stolen property taken from her landlady. On receiving this information Webb only gave her 1s out of the 2s ordered by the bench. He came before the court on Monday 17 February to apprise and explain his decision. Chief magistrate Haberfield gave his formal approval and expressed his pleasure that the conduct of the cotton works' manager turned out not to be as bad as had been represented.[126]

One of the main problems with which Ashworth had to contend was managing female labour. Patrick Joyce maintains,[127] that factory women and

123 *Bath Chronicle*, 17 October 1850, p. 4.
124 *Bristol Times and Mirror*, 22 February 1851, p. 3; J. J. Monaghan, 'The Rise and Fall of the Belfast Cotton Industry', *Irish Historical Studies*, Vol. 3, No. 9 (Mar., 1942), pp. 1-17.
125 *Bristol Times and Mirror*, 22 February 1851, p. 3.
126 *Bristol Times and Mirror*, 22 February 1851, p. 3.
127 Joyce, *Work, Society & Politics: The Culture of the Factory in Later Victorian England*, p. 114.

girls were quiescent but the evidence from Barton Hill is that they actively sought ways in which to resist extreme instances of exploitation and to exert some measure of control over the production process. Carol Morgan argues that Joyce 'fails to capture the diversity of women's experience in the cotton industry' in the north of England at this time. She states that he ignores their involvement 'in the strikes of the 1840s and 1850s,' when 'women played a visible role while joining the unions of the power loom weavers then in formation',[128] asserting that instead they were largely passive and inert and were hardly ever in trade unions.[129]

In Bristol trade unions did not have a presence in the Great Western Cotton Works for the first fifty years of its existence, nonetheless girls and women employed as spinners, winders and weavers displayed greater hostility than the men to management's control strategies of fines, bullying and intimidation. Containing pilfering, sabotage, strikes and absenteeism had from the outset preoccupied management at the factory but the frequent theft of 'inferior' cotton yarn came to obsess Ashworth.

Women and girls were given cops (spools of weft thread) to be wound from the cop onto bobbins ready to use in the weaving process, the crossing of warp and weft threads to produce cloth. The quality of the thread given to them varied so the women and girls were fined if the thread was damaged as a consequence of what was seen as their carelessness or neglect. In theory, however, this was taken into account as, if the overlooker judged the tensile strength of the yarn to be below standard, piece-rates were increased for winding and weaving because there was a greater likelihood of thread breaks.

The evaluation of the overlookers was frequently a bone of contention amongst the women and girls who maintained bias. Consequently to avoid fines from the breaking of inferior cotton thread they smuggled it out of the factory, either dumping it on waste ground or burning it in their homes. A furious Ashworth 'found as much as 20lbs 6ozs, (it was worth 10d. a pound), scattered about the neighbourhood, and in several of the workpeople's houses had seen quantities of the material burning'.[130]

Ashworth turned to the law in an attempt to crack down on this practice. On Monday, 22 December 1851, Mary Cowley was brought before the Bristol magistrates court charged with stealing a quantity of cotton yarn from her employer the Great Western Cotton Company. Cowley was caught leaving the factory with a quantity of damaged cotton weft in her pocket. Her defence was clear and decisive:

128 C. E. Morgan, 'Women, Work and Consciousness in the Mid-Nineteenth-Century English Cotton Industry', *Social History*, Vol. 17, No. 1 (Jan. 1992), p. 24.
129 Joyce, *Work, Society & Politics: The Culture of the Factory in Later Victorian England*, p. 114.
130 *Bristol Mercury*, 27 December 1851, p. 7.

Overlookers and weaving managers, 1899.

If we do not burn it, we do get stopped all our money for it: we do get fined every week for something or other. I have been fined every week since I have been there: we get bad copps (*sic*) given to us, and if we don't use them we are fined.[131]

Ashworth denied the accusations made by Cowley but decided not to press the charge on this occasion if she promised not to steal from the company again. On obtaining this commitment the Chief Magistrate discharged her. Ashworth's objective in bringing the case against Cowley was to use it as a lesson to the rest of the workforce. While he showed a veneer of leniency in this case he made it clear that in future such wilful conduct would 'be severely punished.'[132] True to his word within a month Ashworth was in court again as a prosecution witness. The Great Western Cotton Company pressed charges against Ellen Ware, Elizabeth Garland, Mary Webb and Ellen Palmer for stealing cotton weft from its factory in Barton Hill. Although the local magistrates condemned the system of fining them for being unable to work on inferior cops, they were committed to stand trial at the Bristol Quarter Sessions the following April.[133]

At the same court session another cotton works' employee, ten year old Jeremiah Murphy, was called to answer the charge of criminal damage to machinery belonging to the company. Whether the boy was related to Ann

131 *Bristol Mercury*, 27 December 1851, p. 7.
132 *Bristol Mercury*, 27 December 1851, p. 7.
133 *Bristol Times and Mirror*, 31 January 1852, p. 6.

Murphy is not known but it was alleged that he had deliberately ruptured a self-acting spinning mule mechanism by placing a piece of iron in the path of its machinery wheel that ran back on forth on a track. Ashworth assured the magistrates that the boy had sufficient knowledge to know the consequences of this malicious act.

Murphy owned up to the charge but he said that the damage caused to the machinery was an unintentional outcome of his tomfoolery in playing around with the iron. The court accepted his plea. This came as a relief because if he had been found guilty of causing deliberate damage he would have been sent to the Assize Court where, under the Malicious Injuries to Property Act 1827, a guilty verdict would have made him liable to transportation for life. Instead he was fined £5 (the equivalent of around £477 today), and in default committed to two months imprisonment.[134]

Staffing shortages caused Ashworth in February 1852 to induce sixty experienced factory hands from Lanark, central Scotland, to come and work at Bristol's cotton factory. Twenty children accompanied them. Some of them were allocated houses belonging to the company which they rented for 3s 6d per week. Less than a month later, however, unable to settle twenty families returned to their native home.[135]

By the end of February the relationship between Ashworth and the factory women and girls had reached breaking point. They 'detested' him.[136] Although no fines had been imposed on the women and girls for being unable to work on inferior cotton thread since Ware, Garland, Webb and Palmer had been committed to trial, they were forced to endure a new fine. They were set a minimum quantity to produce each day using the same amount of cops as before. If they failed to achieve the required output they were fined.[137] The company introduced strict precautions in its struggle to reduce the secreting of cotton weft. Women and girls were searched before they went to the toilet as it was evident that waste cotton yarn was being discarded into the draining system. Two men were employed to recover the yarn from the drains and wash it in order to bring it back into production, reflecting the extent of the problem.[138]

The most controversial step taken, however, was the method introduced to facilitate searching the women and girls leaving the factory at the end of the day. Given the large numbers involved, instead of opening the main gates to let the factory hands out Ashworth insisted that they leave first through a door in

134 *Bristol Times and Mirror*, 31 January 1852, p. 6.
135 *Bristol Times and Mirror*, 22 May 1852, p. 3.
136 *Bristol Times and Mirror*, 28 February 1852, p. 5.
137 *Bristol Times and Mirror*, 28 February 1852, p. 5.
138 *Bristol Times and Mirror*, 28 February 1852, p. 5

the mechanics room into the main yard and then, to exit the factory, through a small wicket gate barely wide enough to allow one person to pass at a time. Consequently, this delayed the 1,800 or so hands from leaving the premises by up to an hour. This proved to be one regulation too many.

At ten minutes past six on Thursday evening, 26 February 1852, the women stopped their machines. This action was pre-planned. Normally the women had had to wait until the steam engine had been immobilized before deactivating their spinning apparatus and power-driven looms. What happened afterwards is not altogether clear. Contemporary accounts vary and unsurprisingly witnesses of the event disagreed on the detail. However, as far as can be perceived from contemporary reports, around 600 women and children left the weavers' shed and made their way out through the mechanic's room only to find the exit door closed. They demanded to have it opened. Their ultimatum was only met after they had resorted to smashing the windows with pieces of iron found lying around. They spilled out into the yard. Here they took a stand. They refused to go out by the small wicket gate that they had been forced to use for the previous few weeks and insisted that the main gates be opened as they used to be. Faced with hundreds of feisty women and children hooting and hollering, Ashworth was sent for.

While waiting for Ashworth to arrive an angry crowd had gathered outside the works. Some workers had managed to leave the factory and spread the word to family and friends living nearby who responded sympathetically to the plight of their friends and relations inside the works. In the crowd were 'upwards of fifty men' who had been dismissed by Ashworth over the previous few years for misconduct.[139] Stones were thrown. The situation both inside and outside the factory was described as 'riotous to the extreme'.[140] At around seven o'clock Ashworth arrived. The women confronted him and told him that they would only leave the premises by the main gates and not by the side door. Ashworth snubbed their demand. He brought in two dogs and armed himself with a swordstick (a hollow walking stick containing a short sword). He struck Emma Williams causing her to fall to the ground, kicked her three times and struck her hand with his swordstick. He summoned the works' fire engine and played the hoses on her and all the defiant workers drenching them from head to toe. Pandemonium broke out. There was a rush to the half-open door. Many of the girls fell and were trampled upon. Ashworth struck others as they fled.[141]

139 Letter from John Ashworth to the workpeople of Great Western Cotton Works, 10 March 1852, *Bristol Times and Mirror*, 20 March 1852, p. 4.
140 *Bristol Times and Mirror*, 6 March 1852, p. 3.
141 *Bristol Times and Mirror*, 28 February 1852, p. 5; *London Daily News*, 3 March 1852; *Bristol Times and Mirror*, 6 March 1852, p. 3.

Once the door had been forcibly opened, some of the crowd that had gathered outside ran into the works to give a helping hand to the women and children inside. More stones were thrown and windows broken. Ashworth was struck in the face. The confrontation had turned into a riot. It was estimated that 2,145 stones were thrown weighing an average of half a pound each and 148 panes of glass broken.[142] Assistance had been sought from the local constabulary but only police-sergeant Harman Tozer turned up who, upon seeing the angry crowd of over 200 outside the factory gates hissing and hooting, refused to interfere on the premise that he had not witnessed anyone throwing stones. The next day he was suspended from duty because he had failed to send for assistance.[143] A police investigation into the riotous events followed.

After hearing witness statements, police magistrates granted summonses against Ashworth to four persons and a hearing was set for Monday 1 March at the Council House in Corn Street. Barton Hill came alive and bustled with excitement. On the morning of the hearing between 2,000 and 3,000 people, including several hundred women cotton workers, congregated in the streets adjacent to the Council House. The hearing first heard from Emma Williams who had charged Ashworth with assault. Outside the crowd listened intently to every bit of information that seeped out about the progress of the case. On hearing any scrap of news they vocally expressed their feelings of anger or delight dependent on whether it seemed favourable or bad. After a wait of five hours, deafening cheers and much rejoicing greeted the announcement that Ashworth had been found guilty of assaulting Williams, although the fine of £5 he received was seen as derisory.[144]

The clash between Ashworth and the women weavers and spinners in his employ was of broader significance. Women were at the forefront of resistance against the company culture of bullying and intimidation. Moreover, their actions attracted significant support from the local community and dozens of men who had been dismissed by the company in the recent past. Ashworth's misogynistic and punishing action taken against his female staff impacted on social relations both inside the company and outside in the local community. This resulted in a united class response extending beyond the workplace reflecting the mutually interrelated spheres of gender and class.

However, some male workers employed at the cotton works clearly regarded themselves as belonging to an upper stratum of the working class. Though the term 'aristocracy of labour' frequently resists precise definition Robert Gray notes that a grandiose section of workers can be distinguished

142 *Bristol Times and Mirror*, 6 March 1852, p. 3.
143 *Bristol Times and Mirror*, 27 March 1852, p. 5.
144 *Bristol Times and Mirror*, 6 March 1852, p. 3.

from others 'by their way of life, values and attitudes, as much as by a superior economic position.'[145] Indeed a number of these grandees, male craft workers and administrative staff, rallied round Ashworth. Some of them had spoken in his defence at the trial. They felt strongly about what, in their opinion, was the unjust treatment of Ashworth. On the 13 March an open letter to Ashworth was published in the *Bristol Times and Mirror*'s advertising columns. 110 employees of the cotton works praised Ashworth, stating that his decision to use a narrow outlet by which factory hands had to leave the premises was justified because the company had suffered the theft of:

> large quantities of weft and other valuable property…and all the well-disposed people on the Works are perfectly willing to put up with the slight inconvenience caused by the narrow door, feeling satisfied that it is the means of protecting our employers' property.[146]

The signatories concluded their letter with an offer to pay Ashworth's fine. In reply, Ashworth thanked them for their support but said that he would not accept any financial assistance from them. He added 'nevertheless, this act of liberality on your part will be for ever impressed upon my memory.'[147]

Nearly two weeks later Ashworth was again in court to answer a second summons arising from the riotous events at the end of the preceding month. He faced the charge that on 26 of February 1852 he assaulted and beat 26-year-old Caroline Hill and ordered a large quantity of water to be poured upon her. She alleged that as a result of this attack she sustained damages to the amount of £10. The pleas for the defence were "Not guilty, and justification." After a long deliberation this time the jury returned a verdict of not guilty. On leaving the court Ashworth was mobbed and forced to take refuge in a public house in Old Market.[148]

Ashworth seemed to positively bask in the media attention he had received and acted with callous disregard for many of the women and children in the company's employ. He held an inflated importance of himself that made him feel immune to the consequences of his actions. However, he could only sustain his position of authority through the support of the company owners and many

145 R. Gray, 'The Aristocracy of Labour in Nineteenth-Century Britain c. 1850-1914' in L. A. Clarkson, *British Trade Union and Labour History: A Compendium* (New Jersey: Humanities Press International, 1990) p. 139.
146 *Bristol Times and Mirror*, 13 March 1852, p 4.
147 Letter from John Ashworth to the workpeople of Great Western Cotton Works, 10 March 1852, *Bristol Times and Mirror*, 20 March 1852, p. 4.
148 *Northern Star* and Leeds General Advertiser, 27 March 1852, p. 6; *Bristol Times and Mirror*, 27 March 1852, p. 3.

of the skilled men and administrative staff. Those men that had shown him disrespect were often dealt with harshly, and in some cases dismissed. And those who displayed loyalty and respect were rewarded with higher wages, and sometimes with promotion, thirty-one in fact over his time in charge.[149]

On 30 March, 57 year-old William Fisher, one of the persons discharged by Ashworth, took him to court in an action to recover arrears of salary alleged to be due. During the hearing Fisher also accused Ashworth of acts of violence against him citing one incident where Ashworth had snatched a coffee pot out of his hand and had thrown it at him. Ashworth denied all the accusations.[150] The final verdict was not reported but it in all probability the case was dropped. On 10 April, the trials of Garland, Palmer, Webb and Ware, who were accused of stealing cotton weft, took place at the Bristol Quarter Sessions. They were found guilty. Garland and Palmer were sentenced to two weeks imprisonment and Webb and Ware two days.[151]

On the 29 April once again Ashworth was called before the magistrates to answer an accusation brought before the court by one of his employees, a boy named Ryan. The boy who had been employed at the factory for two years claimed that he was due 12¾ days' back wages which Ashworth said that Ryan had forfeited for being absent after a beating he received from an overlooker. Although technically Ryan had broken his employment contract the magistrates thought this as understandable given the brutal way he was treated. Ashworth, who believed in the iron fist rather than velvet glove approach to workplace discipline, responded that 'it would be impossible to carry on the works without a rule of this kind'. After further discussion Ryan promised that he would return to work and not absent himself from work again without permission. On this understanding Ashworth agreed to give Ryan the back pay he was due.[152]

The diversity of opinion existing concerning Ashworth's harsh management 'motivational' techniques stemmed largely from cultural differences between craft male workers, administrative staff and the rest of the workforce, which were predominately women and children. The differences were particularly large between the highest paid men, many of whom belonged to the Oddfellowship, and the lowest paid majority. Several weeks after the rioting at the cotton works some of the workers, wanting to distance themselves from the disturbances, presented Ashworth with a tea and coffee service bearing the inscription:

149 Letter from John Ashworth to the workpeople of Great Western Cotton Works, 10 March 1852, *Bristol Times and Mirror*, 20 March 1852, p. 4.

150 *Bristol Mercury*, 3 April 1852, p. 7.

151 *Bristol Times and Mirror*, 17 April 1852, p. 3.

152 *Bristol Mercury*, 6 May 1854, p. 7.

This tea and coffee service is presented to Mr. J. Ashworth, manager of the Great Western Cotton-works, by the workpeople employed in the white warping and beaming rooms, and bleachworks, likewise the weaving overlookers, mechanics, &tc. (*sic*), as a testimony of the estimation in which he is held by the majority of the workpeople employed at this establishment, and to shew (*sic*) that they had no connexion (*sic*) with the late disturbance on those premises, which was entirely caused by a portion of the weavers. - Bristol, 12th May, 1852.[153]

However, the regular appearances of Great Western Cotton Company to answer charges of flouting the law continued.

On 15 April the company pleaded guilty to charges brought by a government inspector of contravening the 1847 Fielden's Act by working women and children for more than ten hours a day. The fines and costs awarded against the company amounted to £20.[154] Furthermore, on 17 May seven daughters of one of the families Ashworth had recruited from Lanark appeared before local magistrates after seeking their advice on what they alleged was an act of bad faith on Ashworth's part. They contended that he had induced them to leave Lanark and move to Bristol to work in the Barton Hill cotton factory on the assurance that they would not earn less than 6s a week and that their father, Mr. Hunter, would be given employment working on Ashworth's garden. They maintained that within weeks both of these promises had been broken and that the working environment in the factory was unbearable. Fines had reduced their wages substantially below the promised 6s a week, and their father had been forced to work in the dye works that led to the deterioration in his health; as a consequence of which he had returned to Lanark. Moreover, the Scotswomen complained that the overlookers' conduct 'was beyond endurance, cursing and swearing and using shocking language' and that they were 'kept in the factory beyond proper hours.'[155]

The object of the Hunter family's application to the court for assistance 'was to know what the family should do.'[156] After listening to the accusations against Ashworth's regime the magistrates decided to call on him to appear before them to get his side of the story. Two days later, on 19 May, the magistrates - the Mayor; Colonel Worrall; and J. Gibbs - convened for a full hearing. They heard the testimony of the Hunter daughters, Ashworth and his

153 *Bristol Mercury*, 22 May 1852, p. 8.
154 *Gloucester Journal*, 24 April 1852, p. 3.
155 *Bristol Times and Mirror*, 22 May 1852, p. 3.
156 *Bristol Times and Mirror*, 22 May 1852, p. 3.

witness, Catherine Fabey. The witnesses disagreed on the details of the case but the magistrates concluded that Ashworth had broken the employment contract between the company and the Hunter daughters by failing to give them a formal one-month's notice of his intention to change the terms of the agreement (that is to reduce their wages). Ashworth responded saying that he would give them one-month's notice of reduction immediately, 'and during the month pay them the wages mentioned in the agreement.' The court said he was at perfect liberty to do that and the hearing was closed.[157]

Both employers and employees could be in breach of the employment contract if either one of the parties were deemed to have broken one of its terms. The law generally regarded that such a contract was a union of wills and therefore should be respected. At this time the written contract, if agreed to by both parties, was in most cases the only thing that the law recognized.[158] Each employee of the Great Western Cotton Works entered into a contract to serve the company from the date of being hired until a month's notice be given on either side. On 9 July, William Furnival appeared before the local magistrate's court charged with having broken his contract, which had been signed on 22 January 1852. The prosecution alleged that he had frequently absented himself from work and encouraged others to do likewise. On the 27 June he left without giving due notice and did not return. He was found guilty and fined 10s and costs, or in default of payment, one month's imprisonment.[159]

Even though the law was heavily weighted towards employers rather than workers this was not absolute nor was it completely determined. Sufficient leeway existed for workers to fight for their rights through the courts. Not only the skilled elite but also other mill workers, including women, put their claims forward. So when pushed beyond endurance women workers resorted to violence, but they also spoke forcefully in their own defence with a strong sense of legitimacy.[160]

157 *Bristol Times and Mirror*, 22 May 1852, p. 3.
158 Sir D. H. Parry, *The Sanctity of Contracts in English Law* (London: Stevens & Sons Ltd, published under the auspices of the Hamlyn Trust, 1959), p. 16.
159 *Bristol Mercury*, 16 July 1853, p. 6.
160 On this ambivalent relation to the law see E. P. Thompson, *Whigs and Hunters: The Origin of the Black Act* (London: Allen Lane, 1975) pp. 268-9.

Chapter 6

Weavers' Strike and Breaches of the Factory Acts

Following the bankruptcy of his cotton business in Manchester, fifty-two year old Archibald Vickers replaced Ashworth as works' manager sometime between October 1854 and April 1855.[161] When Vickers arrived in Bristol he found the cotton works 'in a state of utter disorganisation' and discovered that he had inherited a thoroughly demoralized workforce that was well below its full complement by some two to three hundred. In the first year of his appointment he made it a priority to hire the requisite number of people to enable the works to run at full capacity.[162] Some of the problems he inherited, however, proved more difficult to solve. In particular, he soon came to realize that the theft of cotton yarn, as a way in which employees could avoid fines, had not been eradicated by the Ashworth regime.

On 18 April 1855, 35 year-old Jane Driver appeared before the local Bristol magistrates charged with the theft of a quantity of cotton cops from her employer Maze, Ames, Bush & Company. In her defence she explained that she stole the cops 'because she would have been fined 2s had she allowed it to remain.' Vickers the new works' manager told the court that no one had been fined during the last six months; the spinners had simply been requested to lay aside their waste. However, as this was Driver's first offence Vickers decided not to press the charge against her and she was let go with a caution.[163] Like Ashworth had done before him, Vickers used this case as an example to others to show that he was prepared to use the law to impose discipline in the workplace.

A period of relatively peaceful labour relations followed the introduction of the new works' manager at the cotton works. Apart from a couple of prosecutions for stealing company property there were no reported incidents of trouble at the mill for a couple of years. However, following the poor trading year of 1857 Vickers felt it necessary to reduce the company wage bill. In the first week of March 1858 without warning he cut the weavers' piece-rates.

This action triggered a strike. The looms were stopped and when Vickers came to investigate the cause of the stoppage the women 'began to hoot and yell in an extraordinary manner'. This reaction forced Vickers to receive a deputation of three overseers and three weavers in an attempt to reduce the tension and persuade the weavers to resume normal working. In order to

161 *Bristol Mercury*, 15 April 1854, p. 7 and 21 April 1855, p. 7.
162 A short history of Vickers arrival in 1855 as told to the magistrates' court in March 1858, see *Bristol Mercury*, 20 March 1858, p. 7.
163 *Bristol Mercury* 21 April 1855, p. 7.

achieve this Vickers had to convince the deputation of the 'legitimacy' of his wage adjustment agenda. His tactics switched from implementing wage reductions to negotiating a change in the company's pay structure. Vickers proposed the adoption of the Lancashire standard rates of pay on all types of work on the proviso that the deputation had the authorization to represent their work colleagues. Having fulfilled this request, the deputation met with Vickers in the belief that they 'were to have a rise' which would settle their differences with the company over the wage reduction dispute. An agreement accepting the Lancashire standard was drawn up and signed by all the parties concerned.[164]

The weavers returned to work but when the time came to collect their pay they found that not everyone had received an increase, in fact in some cases wages had actually been cut. They claimed that this action was in contravention of the employment contract as due notice had not been given. They lodged their case with the local magistrates court. On Saturday 13 March 1858 the city magistrates called on Vickers to appear before them on the following Monday to explain the accusation made by some of the weavers that he had violated the agreement the two parties had struck the previous week by reducing their wages. Vickers version of events was that only in the case of 'any new description of work' had he introduced new rates of pay and these he claimed were equal to the standard rate paid to Lancashire cotton hands, although this 'standard rate' was open to contention as wages varied across the Lancashire mills.[165]

The question the magistrates had to ascertain under law was whether or not Vickers had broken the agreement he had made with the workplace delegation to settle the strike. The verdict was he had not because both parties signed up to accept the Lancashire standard resulting in some employees receiving more pay than they had before and some less. The magistrates ruled that they could not interfere in the matter any further.[166] In this case the huge power imbalance between capital and labour proved too much for the women at the Great Western Cotton Works to overcome but Vickers did not always have his own way. The passing of the Factory Acts in the first half of the nineteenth century created a basis whereby the state could, if called upon intervene, punish those employers responsible for the worst excesses of worker exploitation.

In February 1859, Vickers pleaded guilty to breaching the Factory Act in a number of cases. He was fined 20s and 15s 6d costs for employing a thirteen-year-old child Henry Dauncey all of one day without allowing time off to attend school:

164 *Bristol Mercury*, 20 March 1858, p. 7.
165 *Bristol Mercury*, 20 March 1858, p. 7.
166 *Bristol Mercury*, 20 March 1858, p. 7.

for employing the same boy without having a certificate from his schoolmaster - 20s, and costs, 15s 6d; Emily Francomb and Mary Fox - same penalty; for employing John Fox, a child under 13 years of age, without entering his name in the register - 40s, and costs, 15s 6d; for employing the same boy more than seven working days without having obtained the certificate of a surgeon - 60s, and costs 15s 6d; for employing the same boy before noon and after one o'clock in the afternoon of the same day - 20s, and costs, 15s 6d; for employing the same boy without the certificate of a schoolmaster - 20s, and costs, 15s 6d; Elisha Young and Fanny Parker - same penalties and costs.[167]

Four other cases were withdrawn.

The company's record over the years suggest that they were willing to take the risk of being prosecuted for breaking the Factory Acts as the fines imposed were derisory. Factory 'inspectors repeatedly complained about the insufficient level of fines' imposed on nineteenth century cotton manufacturers particularly in regard to illegal overworking, which was very profitable. Unsurprisingly, therefore, attempts to eradicate overworking through prosecutions proved to be insufficient.[168]

In contrast cotton workers who were convicted of pilfering were often dealt with severely. For instance, in November 1860 Emma Budd was convicted for stealing 2¾ yards of cloth and sent to prison for six weeks.[169] By this time, however, the company, now renamed as Ames, Bush and Co., had bigger issues to worry about. The British textile industry was heavily reliant on the American South for its cotton supply and as tensions increased between the Northern and Southern States of America, and secession sentiment spread in the late 1850s, the continuity of these supplies began to look increasing vulnerable, therefore the industry took the precautionary measure of increasingly its reserves of raw cotton.

167 *Western Daily Press*, 25 February 1859, p. 2.
168 P. Bolin-Hort, 'Government Inspectors and the Regulation of Industry: On the Problem of True Enforcement of the Early British Factory Acts', p. 41.
169 *Western Daily Press*, 17 November 1860, p. 2.

Chapter 7

The Impact of the American Civil War and its Aftermath

After the outbreak of the American Civil War in 1861, Britain declared its neutrality. This was not enough, however, to stop the eleven Southern states from adopting an informal embargo of cotton supplies to Britain and Europe. The newly formed Confederate States of America believed this strategy would enable them to obtain recognition from Britain and the rest of Europe. They were wrong; and as soon they came to realize that their ploy, known as 'King Cotton diplomacy', had failed, the Northern States of America imposed a blockade preventing cotton exports from leaving the South. [170]

By the spring of 1862 the blockade, albeit belatedly, had begun to bite as cotton reserves across Britain and Europe dwindled. Increasingly cotton operatives were either laid-off or put on short-time working.[171] Although not widely reported the key factor behind short-time working in the English cotton industry was overproduction. The customary way to reduce stocks of finished goods was to substantially reduce the usual number of working days or hours.[172] Nonetheless, the cotton famine that ensued from the American Civil War was the reason given for the dismissal, in October 1862, of over 1,500 operatives at the Great Western Cotton Works.[173]

Meanwhile, the British and Foreign Anti-Slavery Society were holding heated discussions on American slavery throughout the country. It was a difficult time for those with anti-slavery convictions to rally support for the anti-slavery movement not only among the middle classes but also workers, including cotton operatives. George Thompson, an anti-slavery activist, thought he could guarantee the signatures

> of at least two hundred thousand [working class Lancashire women] who are at this moment heroically and uncomplainingly suffering the suspension of our supply of slave-grown cotton, and who are willing to continue to suffer, rather than see the triumph of the slave holder, or a compromise of the principles of liberty on the part of the northern States.[174]

170 F. L. Owsley Jr., *King Cotton Diplomacy: Foreign Relations of The Confederate States of America* (Chicago: The University of Chicago Press, 1959).
171 *Western Daily Press*, 29 April 1862, p. 3.
172 D. A. Farnie, *The English Cotton Industry and the World Market 1815-1896* (Oxford: Clarendon Press, 1979), pp. 144-5.
173 *Bristol Mercury*, 25 October 1862, p. 5.
174 George Thompson to W. L. Garrison, 24 December 1862, cited in C. Midgley, *Women Against Slavery: The British Campaigns 1780-1870* (London: Taylor Francis, 2005), p. 183.

However, Thompson's claims for such support cannot be verified. Working class opinion was rarely reported at this time and the attitudes of Bristol's women cotton workers to the Civil War remain unknown. In general, the voices of the Bristol middle classes were the ones that were heard and the reception to President Lincoln's Emancipation Proclamation on 1 January 1863 revealed widely differing views among them.

On 28 January a meeting was called in Bristol to express 'approval of and sympathy with the anti-slavery policy of President Lincoln and the Government of the U.S.A.' Although George Thompson, the prominent anti-slavery activist was present, it was the local colliery owner and Liberal politician Handel Cossham who moved the adoption of the opening resolution. It read:

That this meeting views with the greatest sorrow the degrading institution of slavery, which has so long held in bondage millions of our fellow-men in the United States of America, and regards it as the true source of the horrible civil war in which that great country is unhappily involved; that it nevertheless cherishes for the people of the United States, to whom they are so nearly related, the greatest sympathy in the present divided condition of their national affairs; and, while regretting that any circumstances should appear to involve British citizens in the guilt of abetting slavery, or seem to throw doubt on the sentiments of this country towards its western sister, this meeting is firmly convinced that the people of Great Britain entertain the most cordial amity and goodwill for the citizens of the United States, and would earnestly deprecate any occurrence which should threaten to interrupt the close fraternity which should ever subsist between nations so allied in language and blood, and occupying the foremost positions in the civilized world. That, therefore, it acknowledges with grateful pleasure the sympathy and kindness which have been shown by Americans to our fellow countrymen rendered destitute by the war, and regards the generous contributions to their relief as a favourable omen, and hopes that the harmonious relations which have so long subsisted between the United States and the mother country will never be interrupted.[175]

From the floor of the meeting the sound of opposition to this rather wordy resolution echoed round the hall. 'Amid great cheering, cries of "Bravo," and hurrahing' Archibald Vickers, the works' manager of the Great Western Cotton factory, stepped on the platform and, after a voice was

175 *Western Daily Press*, 29 January 1863, p. 3.

heard shouting 'vested interest', put forward an amendment that said (with hearers' interruptions):

> While it wished to express its utter abhorrence of all slavery, white, black, or coloured, [it] also expressed its hope that the civil war in America might result in the total abolition of slavery on that continent - (hear, hear) - at the same time it could not but regard the policy of President Lincoln in relation to slavery as partial, insincere - (great cheering and some hissing) - inhuman - (more cheering) - revengeful - (great cheering) - and altogether opposed to those high and noble principles of state policy which alone should guide the councils of a great people. (Much cheering).[176]

In support of his amendment he said that the President's 'proclamation as to emancipation was a pretence … it was adopted for the sake of maintaining the union … if he could have the union he would not care about slavery.' Judging by the applause and cheering, as well as the hissing and calls to sit down, Vickers had a core of supporters present that in all probability would have included some of the better-paid men from the cotton works. Vickers said that he knew the men at his works and elsewhere in Bristol were well read on the subject and 'that they did not need a stranger such as Mr. Thompson [George Thompson] coming to instruct them on the subject.' This brought forth loud calls of disapproval from Cossham's supporters forcing Vickers to retract his statement.[177]

While Vickers' confrontational address attracted 'several hundred hands', when his amendment was put to the meeting, the number against was much larger. The majority greeted the result with great glee. Hats were flung in the air and 'ladies waved their handkerchiefs'.[178] Cossham's resolution was then put and passed by a good majority. However, whether the terms of the resolution can be viewed as unequivocal support for the President is open to conjecture. Moreover, the question arises as to what degree had pro-abolitionists been concerned about the exploitation of working class women, men and children in Britain.[179] This question also applies to Vickers whose intervention reflected the extreme difficulty faced by the Great Western Cotton Company to keep

176 *Western Daily Press*, 29 January 1863, p. 3.
177 *Western Daily Press*, 29 January 1863, p. 3.
178 *Western Daily Press*, 29 January 1863, p. 3.
179 See Claire Midgley's reference to the comments of the socialist lecturer Emma Martin who in 1844 criticized 'philanthropic ladies who wept over the sufferings of people in distant countries while ignoring the exploitation of poor women in their own land', Midgley, *Women Against Slavery: The British Campaigns 1780-1870*, p. 148.

the business afloat rather than particular concern about the welfare of the company's employees.

However optimistic in the hope that hostilities between the Northern and Confederate states would end sooner rather than later, the company did pay a retainer of two days a week wages to those of its employees who had been unable to find alternative employment and were dependent on charity. After several months this optimism turned to pessimism, and in May 1863 the company owners abandoned any hope of reopening its cotton works and withdrew this retainer leaving those 700 operatives, who had not procured alternative employment, solely reliant on charity.[180] Some emigrated. On 29 June, for instance, thirty of them set sail for Queensland Australia at a reduced rate of £6 per head furnished by the *Western Daily Press* Fund and the Local Relief Committee.[181] By the end of the year the works were up for sale and there seemed to be little prospect of the 400 cotton operatives still unemployed getting their old jobs back.[182] The Partnership of Ames, Bush and Company, owners of the cotton works, was dissolved twelve months later.

A few months afterwards a joint-stock company that had obtained a limited liability for running its business stepped in and purchased the cotton works.[183] Following the end of the American Civil War in April 1865, the new owners financed the refurbishment of the cotton works and replaced all the outdated machines with the latest technologically advanced ones. In June 1865 the works were reopened under Charles Frederick Sage, the managing director, and works' manager Thomas Lang.[184] By December, the weaving room resounded with the noise of 805 clacking power looms, and across the works 1,100 women, men and children went busily about their various functions in the production of cloth, including the generation of 3,500 pieces of India shirtings per week. On Boxing Day a celebratory dinner was held to thank the cotton workers for all the work they had done since the reopening of the factory, and a toast was drunk to the success of the Great Western Cotton Works.[185]

Ten months later there was not much to celebrate as the adult male minders in the mule-spinning department struck over the reduction in their wages. The indications are that falling output was the cause for their drop in earnings. The works' manager, Lang, a leading member of the St. Philip's branch of

180 *Western Daily Press*, 12 May 1863, p. 2.
181 *Western Daily Press*, 29 June 1863, p. 2.
182 *Western Daily Press*, 26 December 1863, p. 8.
183 The 1855 Limited Liability Act and the 1856 Joint-Stock Act enabled any group of seven or more people to register as a limited liability company.
184 *Bristol Times and Mirror*, 12 June 1865, pp. 2-3.
185 *Western Daily Press*, 27 December 1865, p. 3.

Hargreaves's Spinning Jenny.

the Conservative Working-Men's Association, had altered the mule-spinning machines to increase the number of turns of twist per inch given to the yarn and, the men alleged, brought into use inferior yarn resulting in frequent thread breaks. On account of these factors the minders said that they were compelled to run the spinning machines at slower speeds.[186] Therefore, they demanded a ten per cent wage increase on the old twist-wheels, five per cent on the new, and the abolition of the 'double time' system. Under this system workers were stopped double-time for any period of absence. For example for one day's absence, two day's pay was stopped.[187]

There is no evidence to suggest that these men were unionized but it is likely that after the American Civil War they had come down from Lancashire, where trade unions had been strong, bringing their labourist politics, customs and ways of working with them. Part of this heritage was their opposition to the employment of women and children in 'skilled' work. This was due to a combination of factors. Prior to the invention of Hargreaves' spinning jenny in 1764, women and children had dominated hand spinning carried out in the home. At first the introduction of the spinning jenny did not change this practice but when improvements to it made it larger, heavier and more

186 See the letter from Thomas Lang, the Works' manager to the editors of the *Western Daily Press*, 6 October 1866, p. 3 and the description the process of increasing 'the twist' in A. Ure, *The Cotton Manufacture of Great Britain*, Vol. II (London: Charles Knight, 1936), p. 208.
187 Leeds Times, 6 October 1866, p. 3; *Western Daily Press*, 4 October 1866, p. 2.

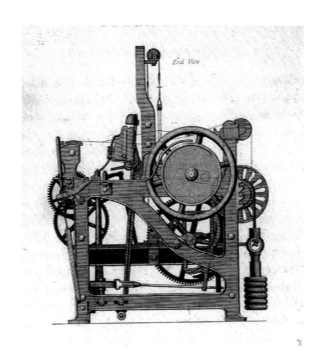

Power loom.

productive it was removed from weavers' cottages into small workshops. With the break-up of the family system, men were drawn to factory employment to earn a living. They took advantage of this change by monopolizing the 'skilled' occupations in the cotton industry as it gave them the opportunity to increase their earnings. In turn this enabled them to raise their contribution to the family income and set in train the argument, taken up by trade unions, for a breadwinner wage.[188] In parallel the transfer of the spinning process from the domestic home to workshops greatly increased the output of yarn creating a greater demand for weavers, an occupation that soon 'absorbed an increasing number of women'.[189]

In Lancashire, by the mid-nineteenth century, male resistance to the employment of female labour had weakened as women came to inhabit many occupations in the industry, including the operation of power looms. Young men, however, had come to dominate the 'skilled/semi-skilled' work of minding self-acting mule spinning machines, a job that became institutionalized enabling

188 A. Clark, *The Struggle for the Breeches: Gender and the Making of the British Working Class* (London: University of California Press, 1997, first published 1995), pp. 197-9.
189 See Ivy Pinchbeck, *Women Workers and the Industrial Revolution 1750-1850* (London: Frank Cass, 1969, first edition published 1930), pp. 148-153.

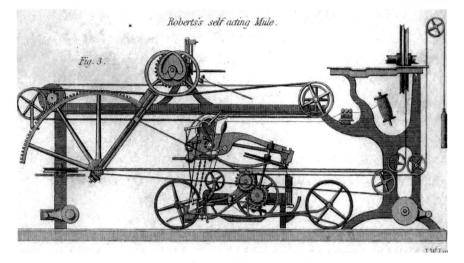

Roberts's self acting Mule.

Fig. 3.

Roberts Self Acting Mule.

minders to exclude women from entering their 'craft' and maintain a relatively well-paid male position in the upper stratum of the division of labour.[190]

No general agreement has emerged to explain this outcome. However, in no particular order of preference, four key factors stand out. First, the greater physical requirements of minding self-acting mule spinning machines for twelve hours per day demanded the coverage of a lot more ground in piecing broken ends of thread than that required on the much smaller throstle spinners which were mainly operated by women. Second, the strength of minders' unions helped to sustain the practice of excluding women from securing minders' positions in the majority of Lancashire Mills, as well as tightly controlling the numbers entering the trade. Third, given their dominant position in the domestic home employers believed that only men could apply tough work discipline over juvenile labour, including beatings, in order to maintain productivity. Male minders who were on piecework were responsible for employing and supervising their child assistants, the piecers (whose job was to repair broken threads) and scavengers (whose task was to pick up the loose cotton from under the machinery).[191]

190 W. Lazonick, *Competitive Advantage on the ShopFloor*, (Cambridge, Massachusetts: Harvard University Press, 1990) pp. 103-4.

191 For a comprehensive analysis of these issues see W. Lazonick, 'Industrial Relations and Technical Change: the Case of the Self-Acting Mule', *Cambridge Journal of Economics, 1979*, No. 3, pp. 231-262 and M. Freifeld, 'Technological Change and the 'Self-Acting' mule: A Study of Skill and the Sexual Division of Labour', *Social History*, Vol. 11. No. 3, October 1986, pp. 319-343. Also see Clark, *The Struggle for the Breeches: Gender and the Making of the British Working Class*, pp. 131-140; Pinchbeck, *Women Workers and the Industrial Revolution 1750-1850*, pp. 148-53 and 185-88; B. L. Hutchins, *Women in Modern Industry* (London: Bell, 1915), pp. 40-61.

Finally, in a challenge to the explanations given above, Mary Freifeld makes the case that minders were able to prevent the dilution of their skill, and hinder women's ability to do their work because 'the introduction of the 'self-actor' intensified 'the mechanical adjustment tasks of the spinner' substituting 'one highly complex task ... for another, while the quality control and mental oversight functions remained unchanged.'[192] In short she argues that reskilling had occurred precluding employers from recruiting low-paid, unskilled female staff to operate self-acting mule spinning machines.

To explain how women were squeezed out of the 'skilled' mule spinners position Friefeld recounts how before the self-actor had come to be widely used mill owners had introduced long and 'doubled' mules. The running of these mules required immense physical strength that 'proved to be a more severe exclusionary barrier to women than had the historically earlier shift to more spindles on small mules from 1780 to 1800.'[193] This development severely restricted the ability of the small number of women who remained to pass on the skills of mule spinning to the next generation. Thus, when the self-acting mule was introduced, and the physical strength to operate them was no longer a barrier, there were too few women trained to take advantage of this. 'By 1849, the 'self-actor' had passed into the control of men.'[194]

No word on the settlement of the October minders' dispute at the Great Western Cotton Works has materialized but the hated double-time penalty was still in existence in November.[195] However, in the following years men continued to monopolize the minder's occupation, totalling forty-five in 1876 with sixty-two boy and nine girl piecers and scavengers under their supervision.[196]

Minders were not the only group to suffer pay cuts. Around three weeks before Christmas Lang announced that weavers too would have their piece-rate reduced in the New Year despite the fact that a little later, at the Christmas dinner held for eighty heads of department, he remarked on the 'extraordinary' progress made by the company since its reopening in 1865.[197] The imposition of wage cuts triggered an explosive outburst of anger from around 200 women weavers who had stopped work. On 31 December, they gathered outside the house of the works' manager, Thomas Lang, in Barton Hill shouting and hollering. The police arrived and asked the crowd to disperse. They approached the most vociferous woman, thirty-four year old Sarah Ann Fear, and told her

192 Freifeld, 'Technological Change and the 'Self-Acting' mule', p. 322.
193 Freifeld, 'Technological Change and the 'Self-Acting' mule', p. 336.
194 Freifeld, 'Technological Change and the 'Self-Acting' mule', p. 337-8.
195 *Western Daily Press*, 27 November 1866, p. 3.
196 Number of staff employed at the Great Western Cotton Factory, 9 March 1876, recorded in the company letter Book 1843-76, Bristol Record Office.
197 *Western Daily Press*, 27 December 1867, p. 2 and 1 January 1868, p. 2.

to refrain from using foul language. The weavers responded by throwing stones and Fear persisted in shouting obscene insults 'and in defiance she came dancing up to the sergeant's face', taunting him.[198] It was common in working class revolts for women to ridicule male authority sexually and to shame working men who broke solidarity.

Fear was arrested along with Elizabeth Hudd and taken to the magistrates' court at the Council House in Corn Street and charged with disorderly conduct and creating a disturbance at the Great Western Cotton Works. A crowd of supporters had followed and gathered outside hooting and shouting their support. Lang informed the Bench that his factory was open and all 'the weavers were at liberty to go to work.' After extracting a promise not to offend again and 'not to engage in any similar disturbance', the two women were discharged and the weavers returned to work.[199] For whatever reason, Lang, it seems, did not take the opportunity to dispose of Fear as the 1871 Census reveals that she held onto her job at the cotton works.

Unlike his predecessors, Lang attracted praise from H. G. Earnshaw, a sub-inspector of factories for the Gloucestershire area who had had the cotton works under his scrutiny since its reopening. He reported that 'a more orderly and better conducted factory did not exist in the West of England.'[200] Nevertheless, in September 1868 Earnshaw obtained a summons against Lang charging him with having detained one of his employees, Eliza Brewer,[201] during her fixed meal break, an offence that contravened the Factory Act. Several other women and children were also found to be working during the meal break but Earnshaw decided to take out a summons only in the one instance. Lang was found guilty but following a request by Earnshaw the Bench applied only the minimum penalty of £1 plus costs.[202]

In March the following year the company avoided taking responsibility for another accident at its works because juveniles working on self-acting mule spinners were employed by minders and not the company. Earnshaw had brought a charge against Mark Anstey, a minder employed at the Barton Hill cotton works, with having

198 *Western Daily Press*, 1 January 1867, p. 2; *Bristol Mercury*, 5 January 1876, p. 3.

199 *Western Daily Press*, 1 January 1867, p. 2.

200 *Bristol Times and Mirror*, 3 October 1868, p. 7.

201 Earnshaw cited in his summons that there was some uncertainty about the name of the woman. The *Bristol Times and Mirror* specified that it was Louisa Bond while the *Western Daily Press* identified the woman as Eliza Brewer.

202 *Western Daily Press*, 2 October 1868, p. 2; *Bristol Times and Mirror*, 3 October 1868, p. 7.

unlawfully employed, or suffered to be employed, a young person named Alfred Summers, between the fixed and traversing bar of a self-acting machine whilst in motion by steam power, whereby Alfred Summers, and the life of another young person was put in great danger.[203]

Summers sustained a fracture of his thigh and the other boy narrowly escaped injury. Anstey pleaded guilty and was fined 30s and costs in respect to each of the boys or in default fourteen days' imprisonment.

The cotton workers in Bristol were thus still employing tactics of riotous resistance into the late 1860s and the dangerous conditions of work persisted - especially it seems for young, inexperienced workers.

203 *Western Daily Press*, 4 March 1869, p. 2.

Chapter 8

Hard Times and Horrific Deaths

Over the next couple of decades - the period described at the time as the Great Depression - workplace injuries and fatalities, wage cuts and strikes characterized workers' experiences in the cotton works, much as they had done before. One particular horrifying instance at the works was reported in March 1869 concerning a fifty-two year old assistant engineer, George Young, who when cleaning and oiling machinery crushed his head between the unguarded revolving wheel of the engine and the ground, killing him instantly. The jury at the coroner's inquest returned a verdict of 'Accidental death'.[204] Dangerous working conditions continued to be regarded as unnatural but not unlawful. In signing the employment contracts at this time employees assumed the risks of all injuries associated with their employment. This principle 'of voluntary assumption of risk was firmly rooted in the *laissez-faire*, free-labour ideology that was supplanting older paternalistic conceptions of employment.'[205]

During the summer of 1869 depression in the cotton trade caused the company to place factory hands at its Barton Hill mill on half-time working. When, on 25 November, the company announced the resumption of full-time operations it imposed a ten per cent reduction in wage rates with immediate effect. At the end of the working day several hundred operatives, comprising carders, winders, mule spinners, throstle spinners and weavers, left the factory and gathered outside of the home of the works' manager, Thomas Lang, and in no uncertain terms expressed their anger at this decree. In fear of disorder the police were called to monitor the situation and 'after several hours the assembly dispersed' with no trouble having been reported.[206]

The following morning these same workers reassembled outside the factory, the women 'flourishing cabbage stalks and pieces of wood' at the minority who refused to join them on strike. Divisions among the workforce were apparent. In particular, the weavers' argued that they should be exempted from a wage reduction because eighteen months previously their department had been the only section singled out to have their pay cut by ten per cent. Therefore, they reasoned, as a matter of fairness, that they should not be included with other

---

204 *Western Daily Press*, 4 March 1869, p. 2.
205 E. Tucker, 'Review' of Jamie L. Bronstein, *Caught in the Machinery: Workplace Accidents and Injured Workers in Nineteenth-Century Britain*, (California: Stanford University Press, 2008), Le Travail, Vol. 62 (Fall, 2008), p. 277.
206 *Western Daily Press*, 25 November 1869, p. 3.

departments in this round of wage reductions.[207]

The company responded forcibly by issuing an order that 'if the hands do not return to work by Monday next [29 November] the factory will be closed for an indefinite period.'[208] By Tuesday 30 November eighty per cent of the workforce had either returned to work or had agreed to return on the following day. Along with a few weavers, some fifty minders held out for a few more days but in effect the strike was over.[209] Sectionalism rather than solidarity weakened the cotton workers' opposition to pay cuts. Indeed, because weavers had experienced larger wage reductions over the previous few years than other sections of the workforce, existing skill and gender had been accentuated.

These divisions led to a piecemeal return to work and were accompanied by a several violent confrontations between strikers and non-strikers. In one such encounter the strikers, Edward James, Frederick Osborne and William Sweet beat the strike breaker, James Griffiths, senseless as he left the factory. His injuries were severe enough for him to be taken to the Bristol Royal Infirmary for treatment. James, Osborne and Sweet were charged with assault, found guilty and each sentenced to two months imprisonment without the option of paying a fine.[210] Other strike-related incidents included that of Ann Bennett who was found guilty of disorderly behavior and using obscene language outside the cotton factory. She was fined 10s and costs, or in default fourteen day's hard labour. William Slane received the same sentence for attempting to rescue Bennett by trying to wrench her free from the police officers who were holding her.[211]

The squeeze on wages endured by factory hands, which extended into the following year, was overshadowed by the deaths of two men in separate distressing incidents, highlighting the dangerous conditions in which operatives had to work. On 18 October 1870, while working in a confined space of only 2ft 7in in breadth, twenty-three year old Samuel Britton was caught in and carried over a flywheel and spur wheel, both spinning at fifty-six revolutions per minute, and crushed. Once the alarm had been raised the engine was stopped and he was found dead lying in a mangled state between the two wheels. At the coroner's inquest one witness reported that just two months previously a man had been discharged from the works for refusing to take on the same work as the deceased had done when he met his death. The jury returned a verdict of 'Accidental death' but with the following observations:

207 *Western Daily Press*, 25 November 1869, p. 3.
208 *Western Daily Press*, 25 November 1869, p. 3.
209 *Western Daily Press*, 25 November 1869, p. 3.
210 *Bristol Mercury*, 11 December 1869, p. 3.
211 *Bristol Mercury*, 4 December 1869, p. 7.

That the jury is of opinion that there was gross neglect on the part of the chief engineer in not having the wheels fenced off from a workman who had to work in so dangerous a place. It was not the first time that a man had lost his life in the factory under similar circumstances, and every care and precaution ought to be taken in future to prevent the accident from occurring again.[212]

A couple of weeks later Lang, representing the Great Western Cotton Company, pleaded guilty at the police court of neglecting to sufficiently fence off the flywheel which Britton was tending when he met his fatal accident. H. G. Earnshaw, who had recently been promoted from a Government sub inspector to a Government Inspector of Factories, and had brought the charge against the company, asked the magistrates to hand out the minimum penalty 'as the company were prepared to act with a considerable amount of liberality towards the widow and children of the deceased.' The magistrates consented and imposed the minimum fine of £5 and costs.[213] However, this was not the end of the case, as later Hester Britton took out proceedings against the company for the recovery of damages for the loss she sustained by the death of her husband. Before her claim came to court however, two further fatalities occurred at the cotton works.

In late October 1870 forty-eight year old storekeeper, Thomas Palmer Hawks, died four weeks after being crushed by a bale of cotton that had fallen from a van.[214] Six months later, forty-eight year old engine driver, Henry Cook, fell into a cistern full with boiling water. Badly scalded he was rushed to the Bristol Royal Infirmary but died soon after. The jury at the coroner's inquest returned the standard verdict in such cases of 'Accidentally scalded to death.'[215]

In August 1871 the Bristol Summer Assize Crown Court considered Hester Britton's claim for compensation. The jury found in her favour and awarded damages of £200. However, the judge, Mr. Justice Brett, gave leave to the company's solicitor

'to move to enter a non-suit if the court above should be of opinion that there was no evidence to go to the jury as to the liability to fence [off the wheels of the machinery], or that he (the judge) should have directed the jury to find for the defendants.'[216]

212 *Western Daily Press*, 20 October 1870, p. 3.
213 *Bristol Mercury*, 5 November 1870, p. 8.
214 *Western Daily Press*, 1 November 1870, p. 2.
215 *Western Daily Press*, 7 April 1871, p. 2.
216 *Western Daily Press*, 15 August 1871, p. 3.

On 7 November, in the Court of Exchequer, the Cotton Company's solicitor, Mr. Kingdon, pursued the leave granted by Judge Brett at the Bristol Assize and argued that the company had operated in complete compliance with the Factory Acts 'to guard against the occurrence of such accidents' as the one incurred by Samuel Britton. Moreover, Kingdon said 'the deceased entered on the employment of his own free will and … he must have known the risks and dangers he ran in accepting such employment.' The Court granted a rule nisi to show cause why a final order should not be granted.[217]

The case to show cause was heard on 29 January 1872 in the Court of Exchequer. The company's solicitor maintained contributory negligence on the part of the deceased. And while he obtained agreement that this would indeed afford a defence, in this case the deceased had not 'the equal knowledge or means of knowledge, with his employer' of the danger he faced, especially given the fact that the task he had been assigned was new to him. Moreover, by Statute there was 'an unqualified duty to fence "every flywheel directly connected with the steam-engine, or water-wheel, or other mechanical power," in a factory.'[218] And although the worker also carried the responsibility of looking after his or her own safety, in this case it was not clear that Britton had been made fully aware of the dangers and risks entailed in oiling the bearings of an unfenced flywheel in a confined space. Whether Britton was aware or not however, the judge said that this still did not relieve the company 'of responsibility, when such an accident as this occurred by the neglect of certain precautions on their part.' The plea for a new trial, therefore, was discharged and the original award of £200 damages to Hester Britton upheld.[219] This case established an important precedent in workers' health and safety rights, the *unqualified* duty of the employer to fence the flywheel when connected to its power source.[220]

On 19 September 1872, nine months after this ruling, another tragedy occurred at the Great Western Cotton Factory. A drive shaft 180 feet long and weighing several tons broke free from the gearing mechanism to which it was attached and crashed down from the ceiling onto the women working below, killing fifteen-year-old Clara Robbins. The physician, William Day, and his nephew, a medical student, Gregory Stock, came quickly to the scene and attended to the injured. Those needing treatment included Martha Vernon (19),[221] who died from her injuries a month later, Hester Gillard, William Ellen

217 *Western Daily Press*, 8 November 1871, p. 3.
218 Cited in Thomas Beven, *The Law of Employers' Liability and Workmen's Compensation* (London: Steven & Haynes, 1909, 4th Edition) p. 39.
219 *Western Daily Press*, 30 January 1872, p. 3.
220 Beven, *The Law of Employers' Liability and Workmen's Compensation*, p. 39.
221 Martha's father, Charles, was an overlooker the Great Western Cotton Works.

Drew, Elizabeth Burrows, Eliza Hunt, Rachel Parker, Ann Cowdry, Elizabeth Garrett and Hannah Hendy. Fifty looms were badly damaged and as a consequence hundreds of workers were laid off. At the inquiry into the death of Clara Robbins held the day after the accident, the coroner, after visiting the site with the jury, concluded that there was no evidence of neglect on the part of the company and that the accident could not have been foreseen. The jury returned a verdict of "Accidental death." Following the decease of Martha Vernon, an inquest into the cause of her death took place. The testimony given at Robbins' inquiry was restated along with some additional evidence related to her injuries. As in the Robbins' case the jury returned a verdict of accidental death.[222]

Just over two weeks after Vernon's death an attempt was made to set fire to the Barton Hill cotton works. The suspicion was that the two events were related. On 9 November a suspect, Sarah Ann Hall, an employee at the works, was brought before the Court on a charge of arson. Forty-two year old John Neale, an overlooker at the factory, witnessed the incident. In his testimony he said that he could not positively identify that it was Hall who had committed the offence as he was too intent on extinguishing the fire. Therefore, due to the lack of evidence Hall was discharged.[223]

In the New Year Charles Edward Wilkinson was brought in from Manchester to replace Lang as the cotton works' manager. He quickly made his mark by replacing the power-loom wheels with new ones enabling looms to run faster. He then reduced weavers' piece-rates by 2¼d per piece which was cut by a further 1½d in early September 1873.[224] Desperate and angry, the weavers struck demanding a ten per cent increase to make up the shortfall in their wages. In a letter published in the *Western Daily Press* they set out their case:

> Gentlemen, - We, the workpeople in the employ of the Great Western Cotton Company, wish to call your attention to a strike which has taken place and thrown about 1,700 people out of employ. When the trade was bad they took about 35 per cent off our wages, and promised to return 10 per cent back, which they never did, besides giving overlookers power to stop some of our wages if we did not turn off (sic) so many pieces of cloth a week. We have asked them to give us back 10 per cent of our wages, as everything has got (sic) up to such a price that we can scarce live by our labour. The company will not comply with our request, and we ask you to publish this, hoping it will induce the public to assist us in our trial. ... [225]

222 *Western Daily Press*, 20 September 1872 p. 3; 21 September 1872 p. 3; and 25 October 1872, p. 2.
223 *Western Daily Press*, 11 November 1872, p. 3.
224 *Western Daily Press*, 12 September 1873, p. 3.
225 The gender of this shopkeeper was not reported. *Western Daily Press*, 12 September 1873, p. 3.

The company responded by offering five per cent. As there was no union readily available to represent the women on Monday 15 September an unofficial meeting was called and held on waste ground opposite the Round Table Inn, Barton Hill, to discuss the overture. The meeting lacked form and ferment. There were no speeches or brickbats thrown against management and no one stepped in to take a lead save for a local shopkeeper who urged them to take the five per cent and return to work 'feeling convinced that the manager would do the best he could for them.'[226] This person had a lot to lose if the strike continued as much of the shop's trade would have come from purchases made by the cotton workers. Yet not all were convinced by the trader's plea. Divided over whether to accept the offer or not the women eschewed making a collective decision on the matter. A drift back to work followed and by Tuesday morning the strike was over.[227]

The situation demanded an organization to transform them into a collective unified force in order to achieve higher wages and better working conditions. Although new unions representing lower paid workers such as agricultural labours and dockers had emerged from the wilderness during the early 1870s, the onset of the Great Depression had interrupted their development.[228] Moreover, in 1874 the founding of Emma Paterson's Women's Protective and Provident League and the formation of the Bristol branch of the National Union of Working Women came too late to be able to play a role in building a union organization strong enough to assist the weavers in their fight against wage cuts. Radical liberal organizations too were in their infancy but had begun to make their mark during this period. Many of the women and men associated with these organizations had a record of supporting inter-class alliances, voicing what they grasped as the needs of poor working-class communities, low paid female and male factory hands and women home workers.

226 *Western Daily Press*, 16 September 1873, p. 3.
227 *Western Daily Press*, 17 September 1873, p. 3.
228 J. Lovell, 'British Trade Unions 1875-1933' in L. Clarkson (ed.) *British Trade Union and Labour History: A Compendium* (New Jersey: Humanities Press, 1990), p. 73.

Part 3 1870-1900

Chapter 9

Women Reformers and Attempts to Organize

By 1870 the Bristol radical liberals, Anna Maria Priestman and her sister Mary, members of Bristol branch of the Ladies National Association, and suffrage supporters, had become involved in the campaign for the repeal of the 1864 Contagious Diseases Acts and the subsequent additions and amendments of 1866 and 1869. Concern over these Acts permeated poor working-class communities, including those residing in St. Philip's and Barton Hill. Medical inspection of women, thought to be prostitutes, in naval ports and garrison towns angered many women living in and around the slum courts of Bristol. One of these women contacted the Bristol branch of the Ladies National Association for knowledge and advice on the subject, following which she set up an information hub at her home where in the evenings many of her neighbours came to read or hear the books and tracts she had received.[229]

Increasingly radical liberal middle class women and men were becoming pro-active in supporting the respectable poor with a view to organizing ways in which they could improve their lives, though the manner in which some middle-class reformers approached women may well have appeared to be condescending. However, it has been argued that the 'Priestman sisters, Dr Eliza [Walker] Dunbar and Emily Sturge among others, saw working-class women as 'voters, lobbyists and allies' rather than as the subject of rescue schemes, and were more concerned with their wages, employment and education than with their morals.'[230] Moreover, they were particularly opposed to the campaign of the Factory Acts Reform Association, an alliance of cotton-weaving unions and male cotton-spinners, in demanding that the Government introduce legislation to reduce women's hours of work from sixty to fifty-four per week in the belief that women should decide for themselves rather than be compelled to work less hours for their own 'protection'.[231] A Bill to this effect was first introduced in Parliament in 1872.

229 The Annual Meeting of the Ladies National Association, 14 November 1871, reported in *The Shield*, 25 November 1871, p. 743.

230 J. Hannam, "An Enlarged Sphere of Usefulness': The Bristol Women's Movement, c. 1860-1914' in M. Dresser and P. Ollerenshaw (eds.) *The Making of Modern Bristol* (Bristol: Redcliffe Press, 1996) p. 194.

231 S. O. Rose 'From Behind Women's Petticoats": The English Factory Act of 1874 as a Cultural Production', *Journal of Historical Sociology* Vol. 4 No. 1 March 1991, pp. 40-41.

In June 1873, a few days before the second reading of the Bill, a leading campaigner for women's suffrage, Millicent Fawcett - later to become a trustee of the National Union of Working Women - wrote to the editor of The Times contending that the passing of this Bill would discourage the employment of women in factories as they would be 'placed at a cruel disadvantage.'[232] Her husband, and Liberal Member of Parliament, Henry Fawcett, also opposed the restriction of the working hours of women and on 30 July 1873 moved the rejection of the measure in the House of Commons. He said that the only justification for limiting the hours of women's work, unless men were subjected to similar legislation, was that they - like children - were not free agents. He contended that the working classes would be better able to settle matters themselves concerning working hours than the state and said that

we can render no greater service to the working classes of this country than firmly to check the growing tendency they show to rely upon State intervention.[233]

His opposition combined with the strong resistance from some factory owners forced the Government to shelve the Bill.

However, the following year, 1874, the Liberal Party suffered defeat in the United Kingdom General Election. Not long after, committed to the extension of Factory legislation[234] the newly elected Tory government, under Benjamin Disraeli, passed the Factories (Health of Women etc.) Bill which restricted the working hours of women, children and young persons employed in textile factories to fifty-six and a half hours per week.[235] That the Bill only applied to women and children masks the fact that surreptitiously the Factory Acts Reform Association, in their agitation for a reduction in working hours, were actually focusing on the demand of adult male spinners in Lancashire for a shorter working day.[236] To have conducted the campaign 'from behind the women's petticoats' was considered as the best way of achieving success in Parliament.[237]

232 The Times, 9 June 1873.
233 Henry Fawcett, House of Commons, Hansard, 30 July 1873, Vol. 217, cc 1287-1306.
234 See W. T. Charley, Conservative Legislation for The Working Classes. No.1 Mines and Factories (London, Westminster: The National Union of Conservative and Constitutional Association, 1885 (LSE Selected Pamphlets)).
235 Rose 'From Behind Women's Petticoats": The English Factory Act of 1874 as a Cultural Production', p. 37.
236 Sidney and Beatrice Webb, The History of Trade Unionism, 1666-1920 (London: Self published for the Students of the Workers' Educational Association, Christmas 1919), p. 311.
237 S. Lewenhak, Women and Trade Unions: An Outline History of Women in the British Trade Union Movement (London: Ernest Benn, 1977), pp. 57-58.

The experience of a generation had taught the Lancashire operatives that any effective limitation of the factory day for women and children could not fail to bring with it an equivalent shortening of the hours of the men who worked with them.[238]

The Factories (Health of Women etc.) Extension Act came into force on 1 January 1875. Within a couple of weeks a series of strikes broke out across the cotton and woollen industries involving both men and women. These strikes came about as a consequence of some mill owners, in reducing women's working hours to comply with the Act, proceeding to cut wages by a corresponding amount. Like some of their counterparts in Lancashire, women weavers at the Great Western Cotton Works walked off the job and only returned to work after the company conceded 'to pay the same amount of wages as they had done previously'.[239]

Anna Maria Priestman took up the fact that the women cotton operatives in Bristol could not work extra hours to make-up their loss in earnings. On 21 July 1875 she formally and forcefully expressed her opposition to the limitation of the working hours of women employed in the Great Western Cotton Works, and elsewhere, when the Royal Commission to inquire into the operation of the Factory and Workshop Acts commenced their sitting in Bristol. She was one of several local 'experts', including the General Secretary of the National Union of Working Women, Henry Hunt, who gave evidence to the Commission. Priestman told the commissioners her belief that the Factory Acts far from protecting women workers actually deprived them of the liberty of working extra hours as

in the Cotton Factory near Bristol, girls had their wages reduced in consequence of working a smaller number of hours. It was the unmarried women who complained principally, as the married could turn their time to account. The single women were "rattened" [deprived of the opportunity to work] by the Government.[240]

Anna Priestman and her sister Mary were members of the Bristol branch of the National Union of Working Women, founded in 1874,[241] an

238 Sidney and Beatrice Webb, *The History of Trade Unionism, 1666-1920*, p. 311.
239 Reports of the inspectors of factories to Her Majesty's principal secretary of state for the Home Department for the half-year ending 30th April 1875 [C.1345], (House of Commons Parliamentary Papers online) p. 71.
240 *Western Daily Press*, 22 July 1875, p. 3.
241 *Bristol Mercury*, 7 November 1874, p. 7.

Women and girls at work in a cotton factory, c 1835.

organization that was vehemently opposed to state legislation restricting the working hours that women could work. Hunt, the Union's General Secretary, argued that the affect of past legislation had resulted in the exclusion of women 'from many branches of labour for which they are especially fitted.'[242] While their opposition to state legislation was in-line with Emma Paterson's Women's Protective and Provident League, there was a noteworthy difference in emphasis. Paterson accepted that the benefits derived from the greater limitation of working hours were indisputable but argued that it was 'difficult to see how legislative enactments can ever be so effective, as measures initiated and watched over by the workers themselves'.[243] Despite these disparities between the sister organizations, they were as one in desiring to improve the lot of working women.

Just two weeks after the Royal Commission Inquiry into the operation of the Factory and Workshop Acts had gathered its evidence from 'specialists' in Bristol, the National Union of Working Women held its first annual meeting at the Workman's Hall, St. James Back, Bristol. On the top table alongside the Union's General Secretary, Henry Hunt, sat the Priestman sisters and two other well-known radical liberal Bristol women, the social reformer and educator, Mary Carpenter, and the house surgeon to the Bristol Royal Hospital

242 *Western Daily Press*, 19 January 1876, p. 3.
243 E. A. Paterson 'The Position of Women engaged in Handicrafts and other Industrial Pursuits', *The Englishwoman's Review*, 1 January, 1875, p. 1.

for Sick Children, Dr. Eliza Walker Dunbar. John Cawsey, president of the Bristol Trades Council (founded in 1873) and member of the Bristol Radical Association, presided.[244]

Alongside its base in Bristol, the National Union of Working Women had established branches in Leicester and Dewsbury. The latter was formed after a successful strike against pay cuts.[245] The women's union gained acceptance from the Trades Union Congress (TUC) in 1875 and sent delegates to their meetings. However, the numbers recruited into union were small; total membership only reached 1,300 in 1879.[246] Walker Dunbar expressed her lament over 'the ignorance of many labouring women' concerning the principles and objectives of the women's union. However, the 'paradoxical situation of women being frequently poorly paid because they were not organized, and protective organization rendered impossible because they were too badly paid to afford even the small sum attendant upon combination' remained a barrier to the effective organization of women.[247] Moreover, in Bristol women workers may well have fought shy of joining because the men were not organized and if the women had formed their own organization an increase in the cases of bullying and intimidation may have resulted, especially from overlookers. Moreover, not to be discounted is the argument that some working class women may have been put off by the way in which the union seemed to talk down to them in a rather condescending manner, as its largely philanthropically inclined middle class leaders tried 'to impress upon working women the necessity of combining in an organization which would tend to elevate their social, moral and intellectual position.'[248]

While the Royal Commission Inquiry was in session at Bristol the self-acting male machine minders at the Great Western Cotton Works were engaged in a strike against a decrease in their earnings as a result of having to work on poor quality material.[249] Two months later, as the economic recession began to bite, the women weavers at the company stopped work demanding the publication of a list of pay rates for producing new kinds of work before their manufacture, instead of having to wait until after they had received their wages at the end of the week.[250]

244 *Western Daily Press*, 4 August 1875, p. 2.
245 Lewenhak, *Women and Trade Unions: An Outline History of Women in the British Trade Union Movement*, pp. 86-7.
246 A. A. Bulley and M. Whitley, *Women's Work* (London: Methuen, 1894), p. 73.
247 K. G. Busbey, 'The Women's Trade Union Movement in Great Britain', *Bulletin of U.S. Dept. of Labor Statistics*, No. 83, July 1909, p. 6.
248 *Western Daily Press*, 4 August 1875, p. 2.
249 *Western Daily Press*, 29 July 1875, p. 2.
250 *Western Daily Press*, 8 October 1875, p. 3.

Low pay and the depression of wages was a constant throughout the history of the Great Western Cotton Works, and women's employment in general in the nineteenth and twentieth centuries. At the end of October 1875, the weavers wrote to the *Western Daily Press* complaining about another reduction in their wages claiming that they were paid fifty to sixty per cent less pay than their counterparts in Lancashire.[251]

Notwithstanding the relentless drive by employers to push down wages, the key issue for the National Union of Working Women was to continue their opposition against legislation restricting the working hours of women.[252] However, the women's union could not persuade the TUC to support them over this matter. Following the Royal Commission's Inquiry a new Bill was introduced to consolidate and amend the existing legislation covering complex provisions including restrictions on the hours and kinds of work permitted for women and children. Despite opposition from Emma Paterson's Women's Protective and Provident League, the National Union of Working Women and Henry Fawcett, the Bill was passed and came into force as The Factory and Workshop Act, 1878.[253]

During 1877 the cotton industry suffered another major cyclical downturn. Demand fell and prices and profits declined leaving companies with surplus stock. Much of the burden of this slump fell on the shoulders of cotton operatives through the reduction of wages, speed-ups and the use of inferior cotton.[254] The Great Western Cotton Works adopted these measures under the direction of a new managing director, George Spafford, and works' manager, James Aspin, who in his career had had five years' experience of managing the largest mill in Bombay (Mumbai), India - the Manockjee Petit Spinning and Weaving Company.[255]

In April 1878 the company imposed a five per cent wage cut citing poor trading conditions for their decision, which the workforce reluctantly

251 *Western Daily Press*, 1 November 1875. p. 3.

252 See Lewenhak, *Women and Trade Unions: An Outline History of Women in the British Trade Union Movement*, pp. 72-74 and M. Ramelson, *The Petticoat Rebellion: A Century of Struggle for Women's Rights* (London: Lawrence and Wishart, 1972) pp. 102-4.

253 Lewenhak, *Women and Trade Unions: An Outline History of Women in the British Trade Union Movement*, pp. 72-74 and Ramelson, *The Petticoat Rebellion: A Century of Struggle for Women's Rights* pp. 102-4.

254 Farnie, *The English Cotton Industry and the World Market 1815-1896*, p. 196.

255 *Bristol Mercury*, 30 September 1878, p. 8. For studies of the Bombay cotton mills see M. D. Morris, *The Emergence of an Industrial Labour Force in India: A Study of the Bombay Cotton Mills, 1854-1947* (London: Cambridge University Press, 1965) and Radha Kumar 'Women in the Bombay Cotton Textile Industry, 1919-1940' in S. Rowbotham and S. Mitter (eds.) *Dignity and Daily Bread: New Forms of Economic Organising among Poor Women in the Third World and the First* (London: Routledge, 1994).

accepted.[256] This turned out to be insufficient, however, as the economic crisis in the cotton industry deepened. Carrying heavy stocks, the company argued that the deterioration in trade, exacerbated by American protectionism, left it with two options; either the closure of the factory or making further significant savings in the wage bill. It chose the latter. On 6 August 1878 the company gave a week's notice of another five per cent reduction. The company highlighted the fact that the whole of the Lancashire cotton industry had slashed the pay of its workforce by ten per cent.[257] Moreover, audaciously, to downplay the economic impact the reduction would have on its workforce, the company raised its voice in disapproval at 'the extravagant style in which some of the female operatives dressed.'[258]

In response to further cuts in their pay, deputations from various departments waited on the works' manager, Aspin, 'to ask forbearance but no concessions could be obtained'.[259] While the spinners and carders grudgingly accepted the reduction, the weavers declined and in defiance stopped work on 13 August. At the end of the next day the Great Western Cotton Company closed the factory.

Anticipating trouble, the following morning a contingent of police met the cotton operatives as they arrived at the factory to pick up their wages. According to correspondence sent to the local press the police acted badly towards the factory hands even though, as attested by the local newspapers, the strikers had conducted themselves in an exemplary manner. A letter from the cotton hands to the local press alleged 'that the wages paid on Thursday were due on Tuesday, and that the police behaved rudely to the operatives, complaint is made of the fines levied in the works for neglect or absence'. The company stood to save £1,000 a week in wages from the lockout of 400 men and boys and 1,300 women and girls.[260]

On 20 August, at a mass meeting held at Troopers' Hill, St. George, a male cotton operative who presided over the meeting denied reports that between thirty and forty weavers instigated the strike, which brought forth a roar of laughter. He believed that the workforce was unanimous in refusing to work at a reduced rate of pay. He then outlined the history of the heightened

256 This wage cut was reported in a letter to the editor of the *Bristol Mercury* from a spinner employed at the Great Western Cotton Works, *Bristol Mercury*, 18 August 1878, p. 3.

257 *Bristol Mercury*, 17 August 1878, p. 6.

258 *Bristol Mercury*, 17 August 1878, p. 3.

259 Letter to the editor of the *Bristol Mercury* from a spinner employed at the Great Western Cotton Works, *Bristol Mercury*, 18 August 1878, p. 3.

260 Letter from the workpeople of the Great Western Cotton Works to the editor of the *Bristol Mercury*, 17 August 1878, p. 6; and information provided in the *Western Daily Press*, 19 August 1878, p. 5.

exploitation suffered by the weavers over the previous decade in comparison with their coworkers in other occupational categories at the Great Western Cotton Works. Not only had they endured greater cuts in remuneration than other departments but also when they were off work through sickness or other personal matters they had to send in someone to fill their place. If they failed to supply a substitute they were fined between 1s and 2s 6d. To counter management claims that Bristol hands were better off than their counterparts in Lancashire, a workman spoke from the floor of the meeting, stressing that Lancashire cotton hands earned more than those in Bristol despite the wage cuts that they had experienced.[261]

The secretary of the Bristol and West of England and South Wales Labourers' Trade Union, John Fox, addressed the meeting and proposed 'that a committee be instructed to wait on the manager [of the cotton works] to resume work at once at the old rate of wages; and that the reduction be submitted to the decision of an independent arbitrator, to whose award we pledge ourselves to submit.' The new secretary of the National Union of Working Women, William Count, seconded the resolution and underlined the collective power that workers gained by belonging to a trade union. He said 'had they been organized, or had they a society to fall back upon, they would not have been called upon to submit to a second reduction of five per cent.' The resolution was put to the meeting and carried.[262]

The next day a deputation made up of representatives of a various categories of workers on strike met the works' manager James Aspin and proposed that the dispute be referred to arbitration. Aspin agreed to put their request to the board of directors.[263] However, it transpired that the managing director, George Spafford was away on business and arrangements were made to send another deputation to wait upon him on his return. On 23 August, the deputation called on Spafford and, on behalf of the strikers, told him that they were willing to return to work at their present rate of wages provided that their dispute would be submitted to arbitration. Without hesitation Spafford rejected their offer, replying that the works would remain closed until the strikers acceded to a five per cent pay cut.[264]

The following week, 27 August, the *Western Daily Press* published a letter from 'a Lancashire man' claiming that in his district cotton operatives were much better paid than their counterparts in Bristol. He said

261 *Bristol Mercury*, 21 August 1878, p. 3.
262 *Bristol Mercury*, 21 August 1878, p. 3.
263 *Bristol Mercury*, 22 August 1878, p. 5.
264 *Bristol Mercury*, 24 August 1878, p. 8.

'for instance, in Bristol their present weekly wages are - Male spinners 17s. to 18s., carders 8s. 6d., and weavers 7s. 6d. for a pair of looms. While in Lancashire the average weekly earnings are - Male spinners 26s., carders 16s., and weavers 18s. for three looms.'[265]

Armed with this knowledge a deputation of overlookers met with Spafford and Aspin and highlighted the differences in the rates of wages paid in Bristol compared with those in Lancashire. The overlookers received the same answer as that given to the strikers but it was delivered in a much milder manner than that handed to the deputation of works' operatives.[266]

Notwithstanding his response to the deputation of overlookers, James Aspin wrote to the editor of the *Bristol Mercury* to negate the message coming over in the local press about the shameful picture drawn of paying the company's weavers and spinners a pittance. In his published letter he set out the weekly net earnings, on a month's average, of a few of the women and girl weavers. From a small sample he found that four-loom weavers were averaging weekly pay that ranged between 16s 2½d and 19s 6d. Out of this wage a weaver had to pay their child assistant, an amount that fluctuated between 2s 6d and 4s per week. Three-loom weavers' pay varied between 13s 3d and 13s 7d. The two-loom weavers (usually operated by young girls or older women) received between 9s 1½d and 9s 7d. In concluding his letter Aspin asked whether there was any other large industry in Bristol in which female labour was better paid? But, somewhat confusingly, in the next sentence he attempted to justify pay disparities with other employers in the city:

> And in comparing our wages with others in the town it must be remembered that at the Cotton Works employment is offered to every member of a family from ten years old upwards, and I could give many instances where four, five and six of the same family are working for us, their total earnings amounting to a very large sum … The only persons receiving 6s. or 7s. a week are young girls learning, and a few old women who are kept to pick waste and sweep floors, work that children could do equally well.[267]

In the meantime, in response to the stories published in the press that the cotton operatives were not being truly represented by their deputation, a ballot

265 *Western Daily Press*, 27 August 1878, p. 6.
266 *Western Daily Press*, 27 August 1878, p. 6.
267 *Bristol Mercury*, 3 September 1878, p. 6.

was sanctioned to determine as to whether the strike should continue.[268] The result revealed that the majority of strikers (only adults were allowed to vote), 662 to 54, held 'firm to their determination not to submit'.[269] The secretary of the Labourer's Union, John Fox, announced the results at an evening meeting at the Coach and Horses tavern, Broadmead. At this gathering one of the women weavers alleged that Aspin's calculation of their average weekly earnings at Bristol's cotton works, published in the local press, was incorrect. She pointed out that the average pay for four-loom weavers was less than 18s 'and out of that sum they had to pay 1s. 8d. for material used in working up the cloth, 4s. 2d. for a helper, and 2d. for doctor, leaving but 12s., which was further subject to fines.'[270]

The cotton operatives approached the Bristol Trades Council for backing only to receive lukewarm support. Its secretary, G. F. Jones, wrote to the directors of the cotton works urging them to accept the offer of its workforce to submit the dispute to arbitration.[271] This plea fell on deaf ears. On 9 September a breakaway meeting chaired by W. F. Kingsey, a foreman at the cotton works, passed a resolution to appoint a deputation 'to wait upon the manager to ask him to allow work to be resumed at the reduction, as, in the present depression of trade, there was little hope of the workpeople obtaining that for which they had struck.'[272] There was no need of a deputation. Kingsey conveyed the result to Aspin who promised him that the factory would reopen within a few days.[273]

This dispute coincided with the opening of the eleventh annual meeting of the TUC, which was being held in Bristol. Delegates from Manchester and London, including Emma Paterson, offered to act as intermediaries to help to bring about a resolution to the Bristol cotton strike. On Thursday 12 September, accompanied by some of the cotton operatives they convened a meeting with Aspin, the works' manager, who informed them that the factory would be open for employees to return on the following Monday. Later in the day William Count and Emma Paterson addressed a packed meeting of the strikers and advised them 'to swallow the pill, however bitter it was.'[274] At first this was rejected by a large majority, only to be rescinded after TUC delegates persuaded

268 *Western Daily Press*, 29 August 1878, p. 5.
269 *Bristol Mercury*, 5 September 1878, p. 5.
270 *Bristol Mercury*, 5 September 1878, p. 5.
271 *Bristol Mercury*, 6 September 1878, p. 8.
272 *Bristol Mercury*, 10 September 1878, p. 5;
273 When Kingsey retired after thirty-three years service in 1887 the company presented him with a gold Maltese cross, a pair of gold eyeglasses, a silk umbrella and an illuminated address, *Western Daily Press*, 20 August 1887, p. 5.
274 *Western Daily Press*, 14 September, p. 3.

them of 'the hopelessness of resistance'.[275] Thus the six-week strike involving 2,000 workers was brought to a close with the women 'smarting under a feeling of injustice.'[276]

The following year the company expressed surprise when its workforce struck work again against a further reduction of five per cent in their wages, as the economic depression in the cotton industry deepened. Given the humiliating defeat the company inflicted on its workforce the previous November, it had expected its workers to tamely submit to another cruel attack on their income. Far from showing deference weavers, spinners and associated occupations refused to meekly roll over. According to The Times, 'the younger and more impulsive of the workpeople' led the revolt against acceptance of the reduction.'[277] The company countered by imposing a lockout declaring that it would not reopen until 15 October when any of its employees who wished to return to work at the reduced rate of pay could do so.[278]

The repeated resistance of the cotton operatives to wage cuts reflects a strong sense of injustice and belies frequently expressed assumptions about women's passivity. They denounced what they regarded as illegitimate reductions in pay by the management. However in each strike the cotton hands expected a softening of their employer's attitude and so were completely unprepared for the obduracy of the company and its determination to push through wage cuts. Although it is hard to probe further into their consciousness of themselves as workers, no evidence exists of a broader awareness of a generalized condition of being exploited as a class. Nor did they hold out any political prospect of a differing state of affairs. It was still the case that opposition to these cuts operated 'within a more widespread acceptance of the seeming permanence of 'wage slavery'.'[279] The operatives did not take any organizational steps to form a branch of a trade union, possibly because of a belief that unions were too weak to make a difference.[280]

A letter signed by 'a poor cottoner' published in the *Western Daily Press* suggests that strikers were preoccupied with their own particular situation, contrasting themselves with Northern cotton workers and other Bristol based trades:

275 *Bristol Mercury*, 14 September, p. 5.
276 *The Women's Union Journal: The Organ of the Women's Protective and Provident League*, 1 November 1878, p. 75.
277 The Times, 7 October 1879, p. 5.
278 *Western Daily Press*, 8 October 1879, p.5
279 N. Kirk, *The Growth of Working Class Reformism in Mid-Victorian England* (Beckenham, Kent: Croom Helm, 1985), p. 301.
280 See J. Kelly, *Rethinking Industrial Relations: Mobilization, Collectivism and Long Waves* (London: Routledge, 1998), p. 48.

There is not a factory in the North where such low wages are paid as are paid at the Bristol Cotton Works. Therefore we feel justified in resisting this, fifth, attack on wages in 18 months.

Some time since our manager challenged anyone to name a firm in Bristol that paid better than he did for female labour. But can anyone name one that pays so little? ...

At the Cotton Works you may see the effects of hard work and low wages unmistakably depleted on the faces of the majority. On the other hand, at other [Bristol] factories the appearances of the employees is neat and cheerful, reflecting sadly upon the under-paid cotton operatives. ... [281]

The cotton works did not reopen on the 15 October as Aspin had promised. However, on the following day weavers were recalled and the sound of clacking power looms could be heard once again. By 23 October, although not reconciled with the company demands, all the factory hands had returned to work at the reduced rate.[282]

The fortunes of the cotton industry improved in the New Year. Production of cotton yarn and cotton piece goods increased by around twenty-one per cent in 1880, and by 1883 output had risen by a further twenty-two per cent.[283] The award of a five per cent pay increase to the Bristol cotton operatives in April 1880 signalled the company's return to prosperity and its need to retain skilled workers, although this advance was hardly generous given wage reductions imposed over the previous few years.[284]

281 *Western Daily Press*, 11 October 1879, p. 3.
282 *Western Daily Press*, 16 October 1879, p. 5; *Gloucester Journal* 25 October 1879, p. 5.
283 W. G. Hoffman, British Industry 1700-1950 (Oxford: Blackwell, 1955), calculated from the production indices of cotton yarn and cotton piece goods, Table 54 Part B 1820-1950.
284 *Bristol Mercury*, 19 April 1880, p. 5.

Chapter 10

Strikes against Low Wages and Attempts to Evade the Factory Acts

Not only were the cotton operatives bitter in the late 1870s. The company's weak trading position during the depression years damaged the pecuniary arrangement it had had with its works' manager, Aspin, which eventually led to his dismissal in September 1880. In April 1877 Aspin had signed a binding contract with the company agreeing that in return for his services he would receive a fixed salary of £300 per annum and three per cent of the company profits each year. According to Aspin, despite his repeated requests for audited accounts so that he could ascertain the amount of profit share he was entitled to receive, the company had failed to release them. Soon after his dismissal he went to court to obtain authority to inspect the company books on the grounds that although he had drawn his annual £300 a year salary he had not received a penny from the profit-sharing part of his contract. The company responded with the claim that during the period of Aspin's contract the business had been running at a loss and that it had kept him informed. The agreement between the Great Western Cotton Company and Aspin stated that the parties were 'bound by the statement of the auditors' which the company maintained it had complied with. The agreement did not compel the directors of the company to release detailed accounts, thus the Judge ruled in its favour.[285]

Notwithstanding Aspin's displeasure with losing his court case he had made a good living during his employment at Bristol's cotton works. A sale of his household furniture and effects revealed that among his possessions he had had a two-wheel dog-cart (light horse-drawn vehicle); a waggonette (horse-drawn and convertible into a Stanhope Phaeton gig); a steam launch with two cabins moored on the Feeder Canal; and five cases of champagne.[286] He had lived rent-free in a large house owned by the Great Western Cotton Company adjoining the cotton works (see the photograph on page 90). Therefore his affluence had been there for all to see, feeding the resentment of the poorly paid cotton operatives who had been subject to his authoritarian, overtly exploitative system of management.

In the first week of February 1882, not long after Aspin had lost his case against his former employer, another strike broke out at Bristol's cotton works. This stoppage was taken in reaction to Spafford's announcement that he was withdrawing the five per cent advance that had been awarded to the workforce

285 *Bristol Mercury*, 17 December 1881, p. 6.
286 *Bristol Mercury*, 16 November 1880, p. 1.

the previous October. The reason he gave for this punitive action was that no corresponding advance had been made to cotton operatives in the north of England.[287] Cotton operatives at the Bristol works contended that their wage rate was at least twenty-five per cent below the rate paid to their Lancashire counterparts.[288] Despite the strength of their case, and the increased demand for cotton goods, the cotton hands were to suffer another crushing defeat. A week after the strike had brought the factory to a standstill a large contingent of spinners persuaded the more resolute women weavers to concede and return to work on the management's terms.[289]

The recurring strikes at the Great Western Cotton Mill in the 1870s and early 1880s, however, reveal that despite the setbacks, the doggedness and determination shown by the Bristol women weavers, in their opposition to management, provides an interesting contrast with the picture drawn by Douglas Farnie of their northern counterparts. He contends that female weavers in the north 'proved punctual, regular, and zealous in their application to labour' and 'they were more docile than men and more easily encouraged to increase production'.[290]

Although pleased to have broken the strike Spafford still needed to reduce production costs while simultaneously meeting the increased demand resulting from the expansion of trade in the early 1880s. A shortage of child labour threatened to undermine this objective which led Spafford in February 1882 to write to the Bristol School Board requesting it to reduce the educational standard fixed by its bye-laws for the employment of children. The committee appointed to consider his application recommended that his request be turned down.[291] However, he was invited to attend the monthly School Board meeting at the end June 1882 to present his case. At this meeting he petitioned for lowering the educational criterion from the forth to the third standard to afford exemption from school attendance for children between the ages of ten to fourteen because 'four out of five who applied for work had not passed' the required standard.[292] He claimed that no other 'town in the kingdom, where child labour was employed,' was the standard set 'so high as in Bristol.'[293]

287 *Bristol Mercury*, 3 February 1882, p. 5.
288 *Western Daily Press*, 6 February 1882, p. 3.
289 *Bristol Mercury*, 6 February, p. 5 and 13 February 1882, p. 5.
290 Farnie, *The English Cotton Industry and the World Market 1815-1896*, p. 300. Jill Liddington and Jill Norris, however, recount that Lancashire women had a reputation of radicalism at work and had been active participants in the Blackburn cotton riots of 1878: J. Liddington and J. Norris, *One Hand Tied Behind Us: The Rise of the Women's Suffrage Movement* (London: Virago, 1978), pp. 61-2.
291 *Western Daily Press*, 25 February 1882, p. 6.
292 *Western Daily Press*, 1 July 1882, p. 3.
293 *Western Daily Press*, 1 July 1882, p. 3.

It was the 1833 Factory Act that had set in train state involvement in the education of working class children. This legislation obliged employers to release children working in textile mills to attend school for specific minimum periods during the working week. Under the 1844 Factory Act more powers were given to factory inspectors to invalidate school certificates if they were of the opinion that these certificates had been issued by incompetent teachers. The 1844 Act compelled children between the ages of eight to thirteen employed in textile factories to attend school for either six half-days or three whole days per week. And following the passing of the 1870 Forster Education Act, the newly formed local School Boards were called upon to make byelaws 'requiring the parents of children of such age, not less than five years nor more than thirteen years, as may be fixed by the byelaws, to cause such children (unless there is some reasonable excuse) to attend school'.[294] In 1880, in line with the 1876 Sandon Elementary Education Act and the 1880 Mundella Elementary Education Act, the Bristol School Board introduced a bye-law that prevented children entering employment before they had reached the age of ten; and only allowed children over ten to work half-time if they had passed the forth standard exam of the new code of regulation.[295]

The Bristol School Board submitted Spafford's plea to lower this standard to the Education Department in William Gladstone's Liberal Government. They replied

> that they had approved in different towns bye-laws allowing very different standards for partial exemption from school attendance, but they were always unwilling to sanction the lowering of such a standard, and would be particularly unwilling to do so in so important a place as Bristol for no stronger reasons than those urged in the letters from the Great Western Cotton Company.[296]

While Spafford's case was under consideration, concern about truant children roaming the streets and causing a nuisance came within range of the cotton works. One week in June 1882 at least fifty windows were broken at the factory as a result of children throwing stones. On one occasion a piece of slate crashed through one of the windows of the spinning shed injuring Ellen

294 Elementary Education Act 1870 (London: Her Majesty's Stationary Office, HMSO), Chapter 75, Section 74, Clause 1. p. 471, cited in Gillard D (2011) *Education in England: a Brief History* www.educationengland.org.uk/history.
295 *Western Daily Press*, 25 September 1880, p. 3; C. Gibson, *The Bristol School Board 1871-1903* (Bristol: Bristol Branch of the Historical Association, The University of Bristol, 1997) pp. 10-11.
296 *Western Daily Press*, 30 September 1882, p. 7.

Great Western House, was owned by the Great Western Cotton Company, was situated next to the cotton works on the corner of Great Western Lane and Glendare Street. Seen here c 1888.

The corner of Great Western Lane and Glendare Street as it is today, 2016. The building on the left, now In Bristol Studios, was originally part of the cotton works.

Little. Fourteen-year-old Thomas Scammell was apprehended and charged with wounding Little. He lived nearby in Corbett Street, Barton Hill. His older sister Ann worked as a cotton weaver at the factory. Scammel was found guilty and fined 2s 6d.[297]

In contrast to Scammel's punishment, cotton hands (many of them children) who had sustained industrial injuries at work had rarely obtained financial compensation from their employer, and even after the introduction of the Employers' Liability Act of 1880, as elsewhere the Great Western Cotton Company was seldom held responsible for such injuries.

> A proof of negligence on the part of the employer was necessary for the employee to collect. Most importantly, "right to die" contracts in which workers renounce their right to sue for injury were still legal and widely used by English industry. Thus, the 1880 law had little effect.[298]

In April 1883, in his continued quest to reduce labour costs, Spafford imposed another wage cut of ten per cent. The spinners stopped work for a brief period but resumed after it became clear that widespread support for another strike was lacking.[299] Some cotton operatives turned to petty crime to subsidize their poor wages. For instance, two girls, Sarah Ann Cowley and Sarah Ann Leonard, employed at Bristol's cotton works were charged with stealing three pocket-handkerchiefs from Jones and Company in Wine Street. Thirteen-year old Leonard lived with her mother and paternal grandparents in Staple Hill along with her one-year-old sister and sixteen-year-old Aunt who was also employed at the cotton works.[300] Both girls were discharged on the assurance that they would not offend again.[301]

By the beginning of 1884 boom had turned to bust in the cotton industry and once again wage cuts were imposed to the tune of ten per cent. In an effort to reverse this trend, in the summer of 1884 minders of self-acting mules at the Great Western Cotton Works struck work for an increase in wages. Fourteen weeks later, October 1884, the strike was still in progress. Hardship forced some of the men to seek employment elsewhere. For instance, Joseph Horwood

297 *Western Daily Press*, 20 June 1882, p. 6; Census Returns of England and Wales, 1881, Ancestry.com, courtesy of the National Archives of the UK, accessed 27 October 2015.
298 G. P. Guyton 'A Brief History of Workers' Compensation', *Iowa Orthopaedic Journal*, Vol. 19, 1999, pp. 106-110.
299 *Western Daily Press*, 5 April 1883, p. 8.
300 Census Returns of England and Wales, 1881, Ancestry.com, courtesy of the National Archives of the UK, accessed 27 October 2015.
301 *Bristol Mercury*, 10 July 1883, p. 3.

managed to secure a job at the Netham Chemical Works, and William Allen found work at John Lysaght's Galvanising Works. However, when their new employers discovered that they were strikers from the cotton works they were discharged.

Following a request from these two men, the Bristol Trades Council wrote to the firms concerned in an attempt to persuade them to reverse their decision but only received a reply from the chairman of the chemical company. He said 'he did not wish to take any part or side in the disputes with his neighbours' but on finding out that Horwood was in receipt of strike pay he felt morally obliged to dismiss him.[302] Unfortunately no more details of the strike have surfaced and it is not known how it concluded except to say that, according to one of the strikers, Spafford refused to accept outside interference such as independent arbitration to resolve the dispute.[303]

The Great Western Cotton Company may not have liked outside interference but it was still answerable to the law. In December 1884 the company was called before local magistrates for infringing the Factory Act. This time it was charged with compelling four young people on 5 November 1884 to give up part of their meal break to clean and oil machinery. The company was found guilty and fined 20s plus costs.[304] Poor employment practices had continued to operate. Moreover, there were warning signs that the company had lost its way and was beginning to flag.

By the end of 1884 the few years of prosperity the cotton industry had enjoyed ended. Trade declined.[305] The company was in the doldrums and once again in financial straits; the threat of closure loomed.[306] It needed an injection of capital in order to compete with its rivals in Lancashire. The number of proprietors responsible for running the business had dwindled over the years, the majority of them having passed away including its managing director Charles Sage. However, this provided the opportunity for restructuring the company.

302 *Bristol Mercury*, 10 October 1884, p. 8.
303 *Western Daily Press*, 10 October 1884, p. 3.
304 *Western Daily Press*, 5 December 1884, p. 7.
305 Hoffman, *British Industry 1700-1950*, Table 54 Part B 1820-1950.
306 Chairman's opening remarks at the Second General Meeting of the Shareholders of the Great Western Cotton Company, *Western Daily Press*, 17 August 1886, p. 8.

Chapter 11

New Unionism and Socialism

In May 1885 a limited company was formed to take over and expand the Great Western Cotton Works. The company was floated on the stock market to raise £100,000 in 5,000 shares of £20 each the amount required for investment in new machinery. Table 3 below lists the directors of the new company who along with friends bought 2,500 shares. However, share applications fell short by £30,000 of what they had anticipated, though this did not stop completion of the purchase of the cotton works and the procurement of new machinery.[307]

The inevitable disruption caused by the installation of new machinery lasted several months leading to the newly formed company losing around £300 in the first six months of its existence. However, the appointment of the former Lord Mayor of Bristol, and Liberal MP for Bristol South, Joseph Dodge Weston, as chairman of the company raised hopes for a new prosperous future. Moreover, his belief in developing 'a sense of fulfilment and contentment amongst the working classes'[308] held prospects of him becoming a central catalyst for a progressive change in labour relations.

By 1886, the cotton trade had picked up substantially and would continue to improve over the next couple of years, which could not have come at a better time for the newly formed company.[309] At its second ordinary meeting it announced that it was in profit and its shareholders would receive a dividend at the rate of five per cent. Furthermore, the meeting supported a proposal to fix the annual remuneration of the directors at £500 a year.[310] However, company accounts for the half-year ending 30 June 1886 revealed that the wages of cotton workers were thirty per cent less in Bristol than in Oldham and Blackburn giving the Great Western Cotton Works a competitive edge.[311]

Low wages helped the company to return a good profit in the following year. The *Bristol Mercury* reported in January 1888 that the Great Western Cotton Works

---

307 *Western Daily Press*, 17 August 1886, p. 8.

308 H. E. Meller, *Leisure and the Changing City, 1870-1914*. (London: Routledge & Kegan Paul, 1976), p. 179.

309 Hoffman, *British Industry 1700-1950*, Table 54 Part B 1820-1950.

310 *Western Daily Press*, 17 August 1886, p. 8.

311 *Bristol Mercury*, 23 August 1886, p. 5.

Table 3 Directors of the Great Western Cotton Company Ltd (1885)

Directors	Business Interest	Political Representation	Points of Note
Joseph Dodge Weston, Chairman	Chairman of the Patent Nut and Bolt Co. Ltd & Chairman of the Bristol Wagon Works Co. Ltd	Liberal Non-Conformist Lord Mayor of Bristol 1880-4; MP for Bristol South 1885; Later 1890 elected as MP for Bristol East	
Tyndall Bright	Partner of Antony Gibbs, Sons & Co. London & Liverpool.		The firm's slave trading activities had ceased in 1841
George William Edwards	Director of the tobacco firm Edwards, Ringer & Co. Bristol	Conservative, Lord Mayor of Bristol 1876-78 & 1886	Master of the Society of Merchant Venturers, 1879
Lewis Fry		Bristol Liberal and later a Liberal Unionist M.P. 1885-95	A Quaker
Albert Fry	Managing Director, Bristol Wagon Works Co. Ltd		A Quaker
W. H. Harford	Partner in the Old Bank, Bristol		Board member of the Old Bank Company
John Lysaght	John Lysaght Ltd. Bristol & Wolverhampton	Conservative High Sheriff of Bristol, 1883	Member of Bristol Fine Arts Academy Committee, 1886
H. Cruger W. Miles	Chairman of the Bristol Sugar Refinery Ltd.		Master of the Society of Merchant Venturers, 1871
George Oswald Spafford	Managing Director of the Great Western Cotton Works		Master of the Society of Merchant Venturers, 1900
Philip J. Worsley	Managing Director of the Netham Chemical Co. Ltd. Bristol	An active Liberal	Member of Oakfield Road Unitarian Church

importance from a labour point of view cannot be over estimated. An immense number of families and a very large and densely populated portion of the city area depended upon the Cotton Works for their existence. The factory absorbs a vast amount of female labour which otherwise would be idle, and it gives employment to a considerable male contingent. ... The prospects of the factory for the current year are highly favourable ... [312]

Labour relations, however, remained poor. Pilfering of cotton weft and calico persisted and once again those responsible were hauled in front of the courts. In April 1888 Elizabeth Marsh, who had been employed at the cotton works for twenty years, and Fanny Hicks, were charged with stealing calico from the Works. Both pleaded guilty. Marsh was jailed for two months with hard labour and Hicks, a younger woman, fined £2 or in default committed to one month's imprisonment, but given time to pay.[313] Petty theft did not seem to eat into the company profits. Following good half-year results at the end of June 1888 the company upped the dividend to its shareholders from five to seven per cent. In the first half of the New Year the company made another healthy profit and increased the dividend it paid to eight per cent.[314]

However, there was no monetary reward for the contribution made by cotton operatives in the success of the company. By autumn 1889 the level of discontent among cotton operatives had intensified. Elsewhere in Bristol workers were becoming increasingly agitated. Union membership among the boot and shoe workers more than doubled between 1886 and 1889. Moreover, Railway men, miners, gasworkers, general labourers and women workers were beginning to organize. The new mood drew inspiration from parallel forms of political radicalism; the formation in 1885 of the Bristol Labour League to promote direct labour representation and the rise of small Marxist socialist groupings, the Social Democratic Federation (SDF) and the Socialist League, both of which linked economic exploitation to the political and social suppression of the working class. In Bristol the Socialist Society brought together Marxists and Christian Socialists. Initially composed of skilled workers and clerks from the late 1880s they gained working class supporters.

In 1886 voters in the ward of St. Philip and St. Jacob's North elected Francis Gilmore Barnett, a Bristol solicitor and a radical Liberal, to the local Council. Although not a working-class candidate, Barnett was a 'friend' of the

312 *Bristol Mercury*, 16 January 1888, p. 6.
313 *Western Daily Press*, 24 April 1888, p. 7.
314 *Yorkshire Post and Leeds Intelligencer*, 6 August 1889, p. 5.

Woman cutters c 1900.

working class and a supporter of trade unions, and was held in high regard by the local labour movement. His brother, Canon Samuel Barnett, was the first warden of the London settlement house, Toynbee Hall.[315] The following year, 1887, the newly formed Bristol Labour League scored its first Council election victory when its candidate, the secretary of the Clothiers and Cutters' Association, Robert Gray Tovey, won the St. Paul's ward.[316] And in January 1889 a local radical solicitor, Hugh Holmes Gore, attained a stunning victory on a socialist ticket in the School Board elections by securing 14,132 votes, the second highest in the field of twenty candidates.[317]

Over the course of 1889 previously casualized, unskilled and semi-skilled workers won several important strike victories. This militant and politically left form of 'new trade unionism' resulted in the formation of the Gasworkers' and General Labourers' Union and the Dock, Wharf, Riverside and General

315 Settlements recruited recent university graduates to 'settle' into poor working-class neighbourhoods to help those in need and push for social reform.
316 Richardson, 'The Bristol Strike Wave of 1889-90' in Backwith, Ball, Hunt and Richardson (eds), *Strikers, Hobblers, Conchies and Reds: A Radical History of Bristol 1880-1939*, p. 93.
317 *Western Daily Press*, 24 January 1889, p. 5. School Boards were the public bodies which established and administered elementary schools locally in England and Wales between 1870 and 1902. For the life story of Hugh Holmes Gore see M. Richardson, *The Enigma of Hugh Holmes Gore: Bristol's Nineteenth Century Christian Socialist Solicitor* (Bristol Radical History Group: 2016).

Labourers' Union. That autumn the number of industrial disputes in Bristol soared. A contemporary described the city as 'a seething centre of revolt'.[318] Over 2,000 Bristol dock workers struck and seventeen hundred cotton operatives from the Great Western Cotton Company, the majority of whom were women and girls, walked out after their ruthless managing director, George Spafford, dismissed their claim for the return of the ten per cent reduction in wages imposed by the company during a trade recession in 1884. His offer to remove some of the fines levied on workers in regard to the damage done in winding cotton thread from the cops to the bobbins, broken windows and access to doctor's records was insufficient in persuading them to return to work. And to ramp up their fight against Spafford they joined the Bristol branch of the Gasworkers and General Labourers' Union.[319]

A new recruit to the Bristol Socialist Society, Miriam Daniell, [320] was blamed for instigating the cotton strike. Married to Edward Tuckett Daniell, a liberal solicitor, she had left her husband and thrown herself into the strikes. On 24 October she had led a deputation of women cotton operatives to petition Spafford to restore their pay to pre-1884 levels. His negative response would trigger the strike. However, according to the honorary secretary of the Bristol City Mission, Charles Helton Tuckett, Daniell was culpable. In a letter to the local press he asserted that

there was not a sound of discontent at the cotton factory until the appearance of Mrs Miriam Daniell.

The morning on which Mrs Daniell presented her demands all the girls had been at work as usual, and it was on receiving the reply from the manager, that Mrs Daniell retorted "Then I will take them out to the last woman." The men as might have been suspected followed in support of this woman.[321]

318 S. Bryher, *An Account of the Labour and Socialist Movement in Bristol*. (Bristol: 1929), Part 2, p. 16.

319 Richardson, 'The Bristol Strike Wave of 1889-90' in Backwith, Ball, Hunt and Richardson (eds), *Strikers, Hobblers, Conchies and Reds: A Radical History of Bristol 1880-1939*, p. 111; Workers' Organising Committee Minutes, 29 October 1889.

320 For an account of Miriam Daniell's rebellious but short life see S. Rowbotham, *Rebel Crossing: New Women, Free Lovers, and Radicals in Britain and the United States*, (London: Verso, forthcoming).

321 *Western Daily Press*, 31 October 1889, p. 3; Richardson, 'The Bristol Strike Wave of 1889-90' in Backwith, Ball, Hunt and Richardson (eds), *Strikers, Hobblers, Conchies and Reds: A Radical History of Bristol 1880-1939*, pp. 112-13.

Daniell denied the allegation: 'I said to Mr Spafford that probably the girls would come out if their demands were not granted' … the girls 'came out of their own accord as a protest against the "starvation" wages they have been receiving.'[322] Spafford had made his position clear from the start of the dispute, telling Daniell, that he would rather close the mill than give way to the strikers.[323]

At the end of October just a few days after the commencement of the cotton strike, the Bristol Socialist Society along with Hugh Holmes Gore and others from the Clifton and Bristol Christian Socialist Society established a strike committee. This body included three new young recruits to the Bristol Socialist Society, Robert Allan Nicol, the organizing secretary of the strike committee, a paid position, Miriam Daniell, treasurer of the strike fund and Helena Born assistant treasurer and secretary. They struggled desperately to support the strikers, appealing for money from women's organizations and church people, though in fact it was to be other trade unionists that would contribute most to the fund. In order to receive donations the Socialists made collection boxes for the strikers. When a letter writer to the *Western Daily Press* asked the cotton striker who had waylaid him for a subscription 'why do not girls go to work? What are you going to do all winter?', he reported indignantly '*Oh! she replied, we are going to live on the rich* (my emphasis).'[324]

Determined to win by any means, Spafford was quick to lodge 'complaints against the police for alleged inaction with regard to intimidation' when the women first stopped work and walked out.[325] This reaction was most likely a response to disturbances that had occurred on 4 November outside the cotton factory gates, as a strike-breaker, Henry Taylor, left the works in Barton Hill. Over 1,000 strikers and their supporters confronted him, shouting and hooting. As he made his way from the factory towards Manchester Street, fifty-one year old widow Millicent Pratten attempted to bonnet him (knock off his hat). This minor 'assault' was perhaps an expression of her pent up anger having worked at the Great Western Cotton Works for forty years in what was at times a hostile, intimidating and harsh working environment. She was bound over on the deposit of £10 to keep the peace for six months. [326]

322 *Western Daily Press*, 1 November 1889, p. 3; Richardson, 'The Bristol Strike Wave of 1889-90' in Backwith, Ball, Hunt and Richardson (eds), *Strikers, Hobblers, Conchies and Reds: A Radical History of Bristol 1880-1939*, p. 113.
323 Miriam Daniell and Helena Born to the editor of the *Women's Union Journal*, published on 15 November 1889, p. 89.
324 *Western Daily Press*, 7 November 1889, p. 3.
325 *Western Daily Press*, 5 November 1889, p.5.
326 *Western Daily Press*, 8 November 1889, p. 8.

Maintaining the momentum of the strike depended on fund raising, rallies and parades organized by the strike committee. Church parades in particular brought a welcome infusion of vigour into the struggle, providing a new way to capture public and press interest. On Sunday 11 November 700 women cotton operatives marched from Barton Hill to the Victoria Rooms in Queens Road, Clifton, where they split into two groups. One group of around 400 paraded to All Saints Church in Pembroke Road and the other 300 to Charles Helton Tuckett's place of worship, Tyndale Congregational Church, in Whiteladies Road.

Yesterday [Sunday] many hundreds of strikers walked in procession to Clifton and crowded two fashionable places of worship and made collections at the doors. At All Saints, the cathedral of Ritualism in Clifton, no reference was made to the unwonted advent of the cotton work girls in factory attire. At Tyndale Baptist (sic) [Congregational] Chapel the Reverend R. Glover spoke of the improvement in the working men's condition of late years.[327]

While church dignitaries remained opposed, this church parade form of petitioning was repeated over the following weeks and would prove effective in gaining support from members of the congregation. Two young and well-educated women socialists, Katharine St John Conway and Enid Stacy, regulars at All Saints Church, joined Daniell, Born, Nicol and others at the strike headquarters in St. Jude's to promote the cotton workers' cause.[328] Another High-Church recruit from Clifton was Gertrude Dix who later drew on the strike in her novel *The Image breakers*.[329]

On the 21 November the Reverend James Maurice Wilson, headmaster of Clifton College, the prestigious boys' school, sent an open letter to striking cotton workers which was published in the *Western Daily Press* and the *Bristol Mercury*. In this letter Wilson heavily criticized the strike leaders for misleading the cotton hands, and stressed the futility of continuing the dispute and urged the strikers to return to work. The letter not only defended the directors' right to manage but also decreed that workers should place unquestioning trust in them, because they were the only people who knew and understood the business, and that they had the employees' best interests at heart:

327 *London Daily News*, 11 November 1889, p. 6, cited in Richardson, 'The Bristol Strike Wave of 1889-90' in Backwith, Ball, Hunt and Richardson (eds), *Strikers, Hobblers, Conchies and Reds: A Radical History of Bristol 1880-1939*, p. 114.
328 Bryher, *An Account of the Bristol Labour and Socialist Movement in Bristol*, Part 2, pp. 22, 29-30.
329 Workers' Organising Committee Minutes, 23 November 1889; G. Dix, *The Image Breakers* (New York: F. A. Stokes, 1909).

You [employees] must leave the judgement of all such matters in the hands of the directors, and when, with full knowledge, with large experience, such men tell you that it is of necessity a choice between the present rate of wages or none you must accept their word...

Believe me, it is safer to trust the word of RESPONSIBLE AND HONOURABLE MEN of the stamp of your directors than it is to anyone else who is busying himself, or herself, in this matter. And you know it so. You cannot really believe all that is put before you in speeches, even though you may applaud it at the time. You must know that the directors are TRUSTED FOR THE MONEY which has been entrusted to them, and they have no right to defraud the shareholders of their just claims for interest.

These are foolish people [Strike Committee] with WARM HEARTS AND WEAK HEADS who tell you that if you only hold out you will win...YOU HAVE BEEN MISLED, as all Bristol knows, not wilfully but in ignorance.[330]

The Christian Socialist, Robert Weare, responded to Wilson's letter on behalf of the Strike Committee. He stressed that the Committee had recommended, as Wilson well knew, that the strikers should return to work; advice that was given purely on the grounds of preventing any more suffering. But the strikers indicated that 'they would rather go to the Union [Workhouse], or to prison, or starve, than go back to work under the old conditions'. He questioned whether Wilson realized that 'the ever increasing consciousness of manhood and womanhood ... will lead to more emphatic protests and stronger revolts against such conditions?' Weare then went on to dismiss Wilson's contention that shareholders must get a dividend of at least 5½ per cent insisting that the strikers 'now rise against it, and say it is no inexorable and divine law, but a transitory precept to which we no longer submit.'[331]

330 Extracts from an open letter to striking cotton workers at the Great Western Cotton Mill from Reverend J. M. Wilson, headmaster of Clifton College, published in the *Western Daily Press*, 22 November 1889, p. 8, cited in Richardson, 'The Bristol Strike Wave of 1889-90' in Backwith, Ball, Hunt and Richardson (eds), *Strikers, Hobblers, Conchies and Reds: A Radical History of Bristol 1880-1939*, p. 116.
331 *Western Daily Press*, 25 November 1889, p. 3, cited in Richardson, 'The Bristol Strike Wave of 1889-90' in Backwith, Ball, Hunt and Richardson (eds), *Strikers, Hobblers, Conchies and Reds: A Radical History of Bristol 1880-1939*, p. 117.

Within a few days of the publication of Weare's letter, however, the strike was called off, though not without rancour. On 26 November 1889 a meeting was held to consider the concessions extracted from Spafford at which the honorary secretary of the Women's Trade Union Association, Clementina Black, who had been seconded onto the strike committee,[332] was present along with Daniell, Gore and other members of the committee. Following a highly-charged debate a resolution was passed by the majority of striking cotton hands to accept the company's terms and return to work. Their main claim for an advance in wages was not granted but as a sign of goodwill the company offered, as part of a settlement, to pay for holidays at Christmas (three days), Easter (one day) and Whitsuntide (one day). Moreover, the company accepted that fines for damage (other than wilful) to windows and payments for bobbins be abolished; that 'the engine be stopped at the proper time for meals, viz., 8.30 a.m., 1 p.m., 5.30 p.m.'; overtime for mechanics be paid at time and a-quarter; that a better quality cotton be used (less breakages enabled windows to be opened to improve ventilation); and that none of the strikers would be dismissed or refused work.[333]

Although these were relatively small gains, aside from pay, never before had the Great Western Cotton hands achieved so many concessions by strikes. Moreover, the women's rebellious spirit was not quelled and the company, due to the loss of production during the strike, were forced into not paying an interim dividend to its shareholders for the half-year ending 31 December 1889.[334]

However, the failure of the cotton workers to regain the levels of pay prior to the 1884 trade recession was seized upon by opponents of the strike, such as Emily Sturge, founder member of the Bristol Women's' Liberal Association and a supporter of the Bristol Association of Working Women. In an address, entitled 'Women and the Labour Movement' delivered to the Bristol Women's Liberal Association at Redland Park Hall, Bristol on 16 December 1889, Sturge declared that if there had already been a women's union at the cotton works 'the employers might have been met, and a fair arrangement come to which would have prevented such a strike.'[335] The Bristol Women's Liberal Association

332 Workers' Organising Committee Minutes, 25 November 1889.
333 Workers' Organising Committee Minutes, 26 November 1889; *Western Daily Press*, 27 November 1889, p. 3.
334 *Bristol Mercury*, 17 February 1890, p. 8; Following the strike, along with the 'disturbed state of the cotton market', it was unable to pay a dividend for the first half of 1890, *Bath Chronicle & Weekly Gazette*, 21 August 1890, p. 8.
335 *Western Daily Press*, 17 December 1889, p. 3. See also Richardson, 'The Bristol Strike Wave of 1889-90' in Backwith, Ball, Hunt and Richardson (eds), *Strikers, Hobblers, Conchies and Reds: A Radical History of Bristol 1880-1939*, p. 118.

and the Bristol Association of Working Women advocated women workers' organization as a basis for industrial peace. They argued that the existence of unions made negotiations possible; seemingly intractable disputes might then be resolved by 'the peaceful work of Boards of Arbitration and Conciliation.'[336]

Despite Emily Sturge's intervention, the cotton operatives not only remained committed to a mixed-gender trade union but also desired to be associated with the militant spirit of new unionism that had been evident in their recent strike. The cotton workers' branch of the Gasworkers' and General Labourers' Union continued to be active and held regular branch meetings in 1890 and 1891.[337]

In January 1890, when Born, Daniell and councillor Robert Tovey were engaged in the arduous task of searching out new recruits from home workers in the clothing industry for the Bristol Tailoresses' branch of the Gasworkers' and General Labourers' Union, the demand for equal pay was made.[338] And in May 1890 Robert Allan Nicol, who in January had been appointed as the Bristol and District secretary of the Gasworkers' Union, won his case at his Union's first delegate conference for adding to the Union's objectives a clause 'to obtain the same wage for women as for men when doing the same work.'[339] Not only did 'New Unionism' not exclude women, it was committed to equality.

In March 1890 the Barton Hill cotton hands were prepared to take strike action again as they alleged that the Great Western Cotton Company had in every instance broken the 1889 strike settlement agreement. On 1 April 1890, R. B. Cunningham Graham MP raised the Bristol cotton workers case in parliament complaining that the works' engine frequently ran over the agreed time and questioned the Secretary of State for the Home Department as to 'why, with the excessive heat and dust that prevails in these works, no preparation had been made for the application of "The Cotton Cloth Factories Act, 1889," which came into operation 1st March, 1890?' Although an assurance was given to Cunningham Graham that the matter would be looked into, parliament did not return to the subject again that year.[340]

336 M. Talbot, *A Plea for Women's Trade Unions*, Pamphlet, Bristol, 1892, p. 6.
337 See Workers' Organising Committee Minutes, 1890 and 1891.
338 Richardson, 'The Bristol Strike Wave of 1889-90' in Backwith, Ball, Hunt and Richardson (eds), *Strikers, Hobblers, Conchies and Reds: A Radical History of Bristol 1880-1939*, pp. 127-9.
339 Minutes of the First Yearly Conference of Delegates of the National Union of Gas workers and General Labourers of Great Britain and Ireland, 19-21 May 1890, Working Class Movement Library, p. 5; Yvonne Kapp, *The Air of Freedom: The Birth of the new Unionism*, Lawrence & Wishart, London, 1989, p. 88.
340 *Hansard*, 1 April 1890, vol. 343, cc 399-400, Factory Acts-Great Western Cotton Works, Bristol, Cunningham Grahame to the Secretary of State for the Home Department.

By spring 1890, employers were beginning to develop new tactics in response to workers' militancy. The workers' offensive began to flag as employers reasserted their authority and the new unions faced pressure on their funds. Nevertheless, employers had been forced to recognize that trade unions among workers outside the craft elite could no longer be ignored. Given this new situation Bristol labour unions reacted by changing strategy; they adopted a more moderate and conciliatory policy.

In early July 1890 the Gasworkers' Union participated with other unions in preparatory talks for the forming a Board of Conciliation and Arbitration,[341] declaring their intent to work jointly with employers to achieve outcomes nominally acceptable to both employers and unions. Robert Allan Nicol and Harold Brabham, represented the Gasworkers' Union with Miriam Daniell acting for its cotton workers' branch. The realization of this initiative came in autumn of 1890 when conjointly the Bristol Chamber of Commerce and the Bristol labour unions launched a Bristol Board of Conciliation and Arbitration.[342]

Despite this shift towards a more conciliatory approach to labour relations by the Gasworkers' Union, its cotton workers' branch remained loyal. On 15 October 1890, 800 members of the branch turned out to hear Clementina Black address their branch meeting at which she gave unequivocal support to the women cotton operatives' preference to stay in the Gasworkers' Union rather than join the Bristol Association of Working Women.[343] By this time, however, the strategic direction of the Gasworkers' Union had begun to move closer to that of the Bristol Association of Working Women, although there were still some significant differences.

In January 1891, at a meeting of the cotton workers' branch of the Gasworkers' and General Labourers' Union, the Social Democratic Federation member, Dan Irving, who had recently replaced Nicol as the Union's Bristol and District secretary, implored the 800 present 'not to rush recklessly into strife, for matters could now be settled in a friendly way that previously had bitterly to be fought out.'[344] The Union's selection of forty-three year old Samuel Bowyer, a roller carrier at the cotton factory, as one of its two delegates for the November annual meeting of the Board of Conciliation and Arbitration reflects the importance it attached to bringing the cotton workers' branch onside. The Bristol Chamber of Commerce appointed Albert Fry, a director of the Great Western Cotton Company, as its envoy.[345]

341 *Bristol Mercury*, 3 July, p. 5.
342 Richardson, 'The Bristol Strike Wave of 1889-90' in Backwith, Ball, Hunt and Richardson (eds), *Strikers, Hobblers, Conchies and Reds: A Radical History of Bristol 1880-1939*, p. 145.
343 *Bristol Mercury*, 16 October 1890, p. 7.
344 *Bristol Mercury*, 9 January 1891, p. 3.
345 *Western Daily Press*, 5 November 1891, p. 7.

**Engineering staff in the main engine house at the
Great Western Cotton Works, 1925.**

By 1891 the Great Western Cotton Company felt once again able to pay a dividend to its shareholders; two and a half per cent for the half-year ending 31 December 1890 and three and a half per cent for the half-year ending 30 June 1891.[346] There was a small sign of an attempt to improve labour relations as well. In April 1891 the Bristol cotton workers' union branch secured for its members an advance of 2½ per cent for all classes of work.[347] And in September 1891, in celebration of a recovery in the cotton trade, operatives were given a half-day's holiday outing to Bristol's Zoological Gardens where they were treated to dinner in a marque erected on the lawn outside the refreshment house.[348]

The New Year opened quite literally with a 'bang'. On 5 January 1892 an explosion occurred at the Great Western Cotton Works just before six o'clock in the morning in the engine house situated in the centre of the factory. The valve of the high-pressure steam chest had failed and, as a consequence, the chest exploded blowing a hole thirteen feet deep in the top corner of the room.

346 *Bristol Mercury*, 27 February 1891, p 8; Morning Post, 6 August 1891. p. 6.
347 *Bristol Mercury*, 6 April 1891, p. 5.
348 *Bristol Mercury*, 21 and 28 September 1891, p.5 and 6 respectively.

A large portion of casting hit Robert Hampson, one of the two men who were in the engine room at the time, crushing his leg. Fortunately, there were no other reported injuries. If the explosion had occurred a quarter of an hour later there would have been ten men in the engine house.[349] While most of the injuries in the cotton works involved unguarded machinery this incident was a reminder that explosions in the industrial use of steam power did occasionally happen which the company would have done well to heed.

Despite the existence of the Board of Conciliation and Arbitration, antagonistic relations on the factory floor at the Great Western Cotton Works were still present and the company continued to use the option of law as a way to obtain employee compliance. One morning in July 1892, between six and eight thirty, nine of the company's women operatives withdrew their labour in sheer frustration that grievances they had continually raised had been ignored. The company took them to court for breaking their contact of employment. One defendant was fined half-a-crown plus costs and the others court costs only.[350]

Unsurprisingly, perhaps, pilfering persisted at the factory. In the last week of September 1892 Mary Old, a winder earning less than 8s a week, was charged with stealing 20 pounds in weight of cotton and a ball of twine. She 'appeared in the dock with a child in her arms, and whose appearance indicated extreme want'.[351] On the part of the company seemingly entrenched breaches of the Factory Act also continued. In the spring of 1893 summonses were issued against the Great Western Cotton Company for employing seventeen women after the one o'clock shut down for a meal break. The company was fined 5s in two of the cases and court costs in the others.[352]

349 *Western Daily Press*, 6 January 1892, p. 3.
350 *Western Daily Press*, 16 July 1892, p. 7.
351 *Bristol Mercury*, 27 September 1892, p. 3.
352 *Western Daily Press*, 19 May 1893, p. 7.

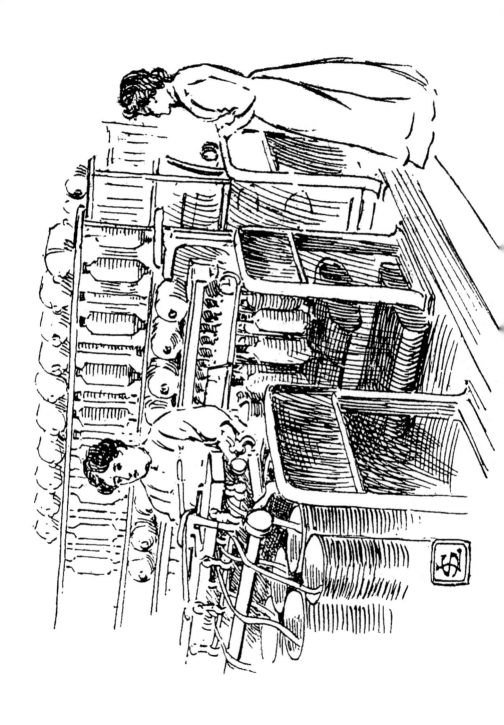

Part 4 A New Century

Chapter 12

Wildcat Strikes and the National Federation of Women Workers

As was frequently the case among vulnerable workers it was left to the state rather than any union to reveal the Great Western Cotton Company's bad working practices. In June 1895, three months after the death of its chairman, Sir Joseph Dodge Weston, the company was charged with not keeping a register of children in their employ at the factory. At the hearing the Factory Inspector, James Maitland, stated that the cotton works in Bristol 'was not at all well conducted with respect to the Factory Acts, as they seemed to have no system at all, and each time he visited the factory he had to find fault.'[353] By the latter part of the 1890s union membership in the company had dwindled leaving only a rump of around forty men (and no women) still holding a union card. In the absence of formal representation the pattern of spontaneous rebelliousness still continued.

The regularity of stoppages of a brief duration reached the point in 1900 when the company felt, once again, the necessity to prosecute the women concerned as an example to others of the management's intolerance towards those withdrawing their labour without due notice. On 15 March 1900 six women cotton operatives went absent without permission from nine o'clock in the morning until two o'clock in the afternoon. The manager of the Great Western Cotton Works told the Court that these six particular women 'were extremely difficult to manage.' They threatened the managers that if they were disciplined over this action they would stay away the following Monday. It is notable that in court the redoubtable Spafford made a plea of leniency towards the defendants. He had not acquired a new softness of heart. He wanted the women to get back to normal working because they would have been difficult to replace at short notice. He told the court he had just wished to teach the women a lesson, one of obedience towards their 'masters'. The women, therefore, were discharged on payment of court costs.[354]

By the early 1900s competition for female labour in Bristol had become more intense; chocolate makers, tobacco companies, stay-makers and paper bag producers, to name a few, were all now vying to recruit women workers. Advertisements for new staff appeared regularly in the local press. Moreover,

353 *Western Daily Press*, 11 June 1895, p. 7.
354 *Bristol Mercury*, 24 March 1900, p. 5; *Western Daily Press*, 24 March 1900, p. 7

Spafford must have been aware fully trained spinners would have been difficult to replace quickly. Spafford was not simply unrelenting in his resolve to protect the shareholders' dividends from the workers' demands; he was consistently misogynistic towards middle class and working class women alike. He was also profoundly authoritarian. He vehemently opposed women's suffrage, for instance, in the belief that women by nature were inferior to men. In a letter to the editor of the *Western Daily Press* in December 1909 he envisioned the possibility of a House of Commons composed entirely of women prompting the question - 'Is it conceivable that men, the superior force, would submit to laws made by women?'[355]

On 27 June 1900 yet again several women from the Barton Hill cotton works were brought before the local magistrates charged with stopping work for two and half hours on 14 June, and nearly two hours on 15 June, without giving due notice. The defence they offered was that the material they were given to work on was 'bad'. They had no desire to quit the company they just objected to having to work with inferior cotton yarn. Spafford complained that 'it was very difficult to continue the work in consequence of the independence of the workers.' Even in the days immediately preceding the court case 'these same spinners had stopped work at least twenty times' in spite of warnings. The case was adjourned for six weeks in the hope that the problem would be solved in house.[356]

Despite the lack of union involvement in stoppages carried out by rebellious women, the management of Bristol's cotton works seemed unable to deal with them without the assistance of the courts. The following year more stoppages occurred. In October, five young women were charged with breaking their contract of employment. Just a few months previously three of the defendants had appeared before the court for a similar offence. These women were fined 10s and costs, the other two 3s without costs.[357] Corresponding offences occurred again in January 1903 when Ellen Trotman, Alice House, Eliza Pincott, Maggie Heath, Maud Sawyer and Elizabeth Lewis, all single women aged between twenty and twenty-six years of age, were charged with having broken their contracts of employment with the Great Western Cotton Company.[358] During this period Spafford was clearly struggling to maintain discipline in the factory which no doubt intensified his contempt for the women under his authority.

In the New Year the cotton trade began to slide into a recession once again. As a consequence the directors of the Barton Hill cotton works announced

355 *Western Daily Press*, 10 December 1909, p. 3.
356 *Western Daily Press*, 28 June 1900, p. 6.
357 *Western Daily Press*, 1 October 1901, p. 7.
358 *Western Daily Press*, 20 January 1903, p. 9.

on Wednesday 27 January that the factory would close until the following Tuesday. There was an angry reaction. At midday, immediately following this announcement, a 'disorderly' crowd of cotton workers gathered outside the house of the works' manager in protest telling him what they thought in no uncertain terms. Soon after the police arrived to restore order and the crowd dispersed.[359]

By Easter the continued fall in trade caused the directors of the cotton works to impose a wage cut of five per cent. In May the company announced a further five per cent reduction. This time the 1,000 strong workforce refused to accept this new assault on their living standards and as a result they were locked out.[360] Harold Brabham, the local secretary of the Gasworkers and General Labourers' Union was called upon to assist even though only forty cotton workers employed at the factory held a union card. At a special meeting of the men in the Rhubarb Tavern, Queen Ann Road, Barton Hill, it was decided to send a deputation to wait on Spafford to see if a compromise could be reached. The men came back empty handed, as a result a meeting of the whole workforce was called.

Around 1,000 cotton hands assembled to hear Brabham. Perhaps somewhat over-optimistically, he reminded those present that several years previously, when most of the cotton operatives had belonged to the union, 'they were always able to overcome any difficulties that had arisen without the slightest hitch.' A resolution was then put urging the whole of the workforce to join the union which was carried unanimously. The men signed up immediately. The women held back, although they too were vehemently opposed to the pay cuts. The union campaigned on the principle that if the factory was fully unionized industrial peace would likely follow. It recognized that the cotton industry was in recession and that a wage cut might be necessary, but it argued that the workforce should be consulted over the extent and terms of such a discordant measure.[361]

A compromise - based on accepting the five per cent reduction provided that it would be restored on 1 September 1904 and a further two and a half per cent of the Easter cut returned on 1 January 1905 - was put to Spafford.[362] Although this offer was rejected a conciliatory Brabham was at pains to point out that agreement was close and that Spafford 'was not like some employers who would not see a paid secretary of the union. On the contrary he treated him [Mr Brabham] as a gentleman and he should always be prepared to treat

359 *Western Daily Press*, 29 January 1904, p. 9.
360 *Western Daily Press*, 21 May 1904, p. 5.
361 *Western Daily Press*, 27 May, p. 7 and 28 May 1904, p. 9.
362 *Western Daily Press*, 28 May 1904, p. 9.

Mr Spafford the same.'[363] This was the same George Spafford that 'was reputed to have said "that he would rather burn the mill rather than concede" to his workers' demands in the 1889 strike.'[364]

The lockout ended on 1 June 1904. After a vote by the workforce the five per cent wage reduction was accepted on the company's assurance that it would be restored, provided the depression in the cotton industry eased, at the end of September.[365] Following the resolution of this dispute a significant number of male and female cotton hands joined the Gasworkers' Union persuaded by the argument that as a united body they would be more likely to get their grievances addressed once the industry had come out of recession.

The business continued to struggle, however. Again on several occasions the company was exposed for breaking the Factory Act by making women work past the set time for their meal break.[366] In July 1905 the Great Western Cotton Company petitioned the Chancery Division of the High Court of Justice to obtain the sanction of the court to reduce the capital of the company from £150,000 to £110,000 in order to put the company 'on a sound and dividend-earning footing.' The court assented to the petition.[367]

The company had another problem with which to contend - more wildcat strikes. Following the settlement of one such stoppage, in which winders had ceased work in support of a colleague who had been dismissed,[368] a special meeting of the Cotton Workers' branch of the Gasworkers' and General Labourers' Union was called. The meeting, held on 21 September 1906, was given over to the union's concern about sudden stoppages of work at the factory without notice and without informing the union.

E. J. Burt, chairman of the Bristol Trades Council, presided. Several prominent union leaders - including the General Secretary of the Gasworkers' Union, Will Thorne MP, and the union's national organizer, Pete Curran - spoke against the practice of unofficial industrial action. Curran's message was clear, members he said must submit to trade union rules and discipline. Moreover, 'the union did not recognize any dispute where the workers immediately left their employment without notifying the local officers of the union.' Thorne concurred with Curran and told the meeting that when any future dispute arose members should send for the local union secretary, Harold Brabham, to deal with the matter. 'He urged them not to act as they did before.' Notwithstanding

363 *Western Daily Press*, 30 May 1904, p. 5.
364 See Richardson, 'The Bristol Strike Wave of 1889-90' in Backwith, Ball, Hunt and Richardson (eds), *Strikers, Hobblers, Conchies and Reds: A Radical History of Bristol 1880-1939*, p. 113.
365 *Western Daily Press*, 1 June 1904.
366 *Western Daily Press*, 22 December 1904, p. 9.
367 *Western Daily Press*, 10 July 1905, p. 10.
368 *Western Daily Press*, 15 September 1906, p. 5.

the union officials' censoriousness the meeting closed with the announcement that the Bristol cotton workers would receive strike pay for their recent five-day unauthorized stoppage, which was greeted by cheers of approval.[369]

The union leaders, however, as well as damning wildcat strikes had held a meeting with Spafford 'who met them in a cordial spirit.' Curran hastened to assure the workers that as a result of this meeting a better understanding between employees and management would emerge. [370] The officials' denunciation of wildcat action was particularly directed at the women spinners and weavers, who not only had been the main participants in spontaneous strikes but also had suffered most under Spafford's regime. It is not surprising therefore to find that over time the women's trust in the union would begin to wane.

By the end of 1907 union membership among women spinners, winders and weavers at the Great Western Cotton Factory had collapsed. And yet between January and mid-November 1907 women winders had on eight occasions ceased work without notice. Each time the factory was brought to an unscheduled standstill. The company decided to sue them for damages after thirty-four winders on the 1, 2 and 4 November stopped their machines again for two or three hours at a time in protest against having to work with inferior cotton thread. These women were on piecework and having to wind brittle yarn had effected a reduction in their income which was already pitifully low. The unofficial stoppages were marked by a brief joyous freedom. The company was particularly outraged at the women's defiant attitude in remaining in the winders' room 'singing and laughing throughout the day.' As a consequence of their actions the company claimed that the cost it entailed, due to the loss of production, amounted to at least £200.[371]

In court it was confirmed that indeed the thread that the winders had been expected to use was inferior and that a deputation represented by all departments had waited on the manager complaining about this problem. However, as their defence solicitor, a former member of the Bristol Socialist Society, Edward Watson, admitted the winders had broken their employment contract but he implored the court not to set the damages too high due to the low wages of the defendants. After the court had heard that the winders intended to return to work, they were each fined 5s damages and 2s costs to be paid in weekly installments. A crowd of factory women and girls large enough to disrupt the traffic greeted the defendants as they left the court.[372]

In an attempt to break the winders' strike yarn was brought in from

369 *Western Daily Press*, 22 September 1906, p. 9.
370 *Western Daily Press*, 22 September 1906, p. 9.
371 *Western Daily Press*, 16 November 1907, p. 8.
372 *Western Daily Press*, 16 November 1907, p. 8.

Lancashire. This yarn had to be sized prior to weaving. This was the job of the drawers. On 1 January 1908 the Great Western Cotton Company was summonsed for infringing the Factory Act by countenancing fifteen women drawers on one occasion to work through their half-an-hour meal break, and a boy once during the tea break and twice after hours at night. The factory inspector highlighted the fact that the company had violated the Factory Act on many previous occasions. The company pleaded guilty to a technical offence and was fined.[373]

Intervention by the courts, however, did little to stop disruption at the cotton works, and neither did the condemnation by the trade unions against the continued practice of illegal stoppages have any effect. In desperation the company directors issued a written statement to its workpeople warning them that if the sectional strike persisted the works could well have to close (see appendix 1 'To the Workpeople'): But as it turned out it was the decline in orders that resulted in the company suspending production.

At the end of August 1908 the factory closed for five days owing to the depression in trade, throwing 1,700 cotton operatives out of work.[374] The shortage of work continued throughout the following year. In December 1909 a fund was established to open a soup kitchen in Barton Hill to help those of the 500 or so cotton workers in the most need. It is somewhat ironic that the early subscribers to this fund included the Great Western Cotton Company (£100) and its managing director Spafford (£50).[375] For laid-off workers the prospect of a merry Christmas seemed remote. A Christmas dinner provided by charity was the best many of them could hope for.

The cotton trade began a slow recovery over the next couple of years and in March 1913 the directors of Great Western Cotton Company recommended a dividend of fifteen per cent on preference shares, which would clear all arrears, and two and a half per cent on ordinary shares.[376] Its workforce, however, amidst widespread labour unrest nationally, began to show signs of discontent once again.

On 14 April 1913 the age-old problem of being compelled to use sub-standard yarn led to a strike by twenty-four women winders.[377] The following

373 *Western Daily Press*, 2 January 1908, p. 7.
374 *Western Daily Press*, 31 August, p. 5 and 5 September 1908, p. 12.
375 *Western Daily Press*, 10 December 1909, p. 5.
376 *Aberdeen Journal*, 15 March 1913, p. 9.
377 The defendants' names were published in the *Western Daily Press*, 15 April 1913, p.7. They are as follows: Rebecca Darby, Florence Baily, Mary Ann Lawler, Susan Gingell, Amy Pavey, Polly Stowell, Lydia White, Annie White, Alice Wiltshire, Rose Sherring, Ellen Iles, Jane Lucas, Emily White, Maltilda Gregory, Alice Jennings, Blanche Pullin, Violet Jenkins, Louisa Gardiner, Kate Gordon, Lily Brown, Alice Edwards, Grace Clothier, Rose Taft and Charlotte White.

day they appeared before the local magistrate court charged with breaching their contract of employment with the Great Western Cotton Company. Called to the witness box, George Spafford, still managing director, intimated that it was not inferior cotton yarn that reduced the ability of the women, who were paid by the piece, to earn as much money as they had before but idleness. He accused them of 'malingering'. The women were all found guilty and each defendant was ordered to pay a fine of 2s and 1s costs.[378] Profits made by the company during the year enabled the company to pay its shareholders five per cent for the twelve months ending 31 December 1913,[379] a period when women weavers' earnings in Bristol were 'below the minimum rates fixed about that time for "sweated" workers under the Trade Boards Act.'[380]

Just over six months later eighty spinners employed at the Great Western Cotton Works struck work for an advance in pay. The National Federation of Women Workers (NFWW), under the leadership of Mary Macarthur, stepped in to support these women. They had been without union representation for several years, and were among the lowest paid in the country with earnings of no more than 9s a week. They joined the NFWW who immediately opened negotiations with the company on the strikers' behalf. The NFWW obtained what they described as a 'considerable advance' in the piece-rate that 'made a difference of a couple of shillings advance in the wages of those engaged on that work.'[381] Within days a further 400 women had signed up with the union.

Quick to build on this success with the support of the Bristol Trades Council the NFWW called on Bristol's women cotton workers to attend a recruitment meeting on 14 July in Redfield, around three quarters of a mile from the cotton factory. One of the union's full-time organizers, Miss Vickers, addressed this meeting remarking that the Great Western Cotton Company 'was one of the worst she had had to deal with.' However, 'she did not wish them [cotton workers] to strike, because she realized that they could ill afford to lose a day's work, and she hoped there would be no further trouble, and that they would encourage all their fellow workers to come into the Union.' A second speaker, another NFWW organizer, Barbara Keen, advised that having won their dispute the women should be satisfied for the moment 'and bide their time.'[382] The recruitment drive finished with those present pledging 'to remain members of the National Federation of Women Workers, firmly believing that

---

378 *Western Daily Press*, 15 April 1913, p. 7.
379 *Manchester Courier & Lancashire General Advertiser*, 7 March 1914, p. 4.
380 B. Drake, *Women in Trade Unions* (London: Virago, 1984, first published 1920 by the Labour Research Department), p. 51.
381 *Western Daily Press*, 15 July 1914, p. 11.
382 *Western Daily Press*, 15 July 1914, p. 11.

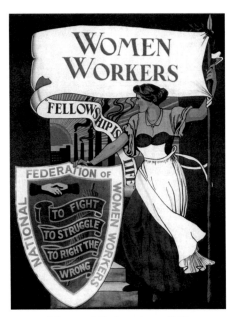

National Federation of Women Workers banner.

only by combined efforts can our condition, both in the matter of wages and hours, be improved.'[383] A few months later war between Britain and Germany was declared, one of its unintended consequences would be to significantly alter the position of women workers.

The following memoir of Flo Melhuish suggests that the experience of war did little to quell the indomitable spirit of girls and young women working in Barton Hill. Yet the contradiction between needing a job and the will to resist the worst excesses of exploitation was as evident then as it is now.

At fourteen years of age Flo started work in the weaving shed at the Great Western Cotton Works:

I was only there for a few days, that was before Xmas. I thought I was doing well. I was told I was doing alright. So the woman in charge said she was going down the pub to have a drink, she wouldn't be very long, and would I go on with the job. So I said 'Yes to the best of my ability I will.' If you remember I'm only fourteen. So away she goes to the pub and I gets on with the machine.

When she comes back she finds this long streak down the calico. 'Oh' she said, 'what's that, how long has that been going on?' So I said, 'for some time. What's the Trouble?' She said, 'That's bad work, I don't get paid for none of that. All that's got to be taken off and re-weaved.' So I said, 'I'm awfully sorry. 'I apologized to her. I said 'I thought I was doing my best.' When all's said, she got in a temper, slapped my face and left her fingermarks on my face. So I thought, well the only thing I can do now is to give her one back. So I picked up the bobbin and let her have one back see. So the foreman says, 'What's going on here?' So I said, 'Well, she slapped me across the face, you can still see the marks. I got into a bit of a paddy and hit her one with the bobbin.

So he said, 'That's enough of that then. You go to the office and get your cards. You're finished.'[384]

After Christmas Flo tried to find other employment without success, so she went back to the cotton factory and approached the spinning room foreman, Alfred Clark for a job. He said that there were no vacancies. She cried. One of the managers, 'Spafford' - most likely to have been thirty-two year old Arthur Miles Spafford, the nephew of the previous manager, George Oswald Spafford - arrived on the scene to see what was going on. Flo turned to him and, appealing to his better nature, said:

'I've been in to ask Mr. Clark if he'd give me a job and you've got no work there, and I can't go home and tell my dad. He's an invalid and we've got seven children to keep, and we could do with the money.'

So he listens to my story and he says, 'What regiment was your dad in?' I said. 'Somerset Light Infantry.'

He said, 'So was I. Alright come into the office with me and see Alfie Clark. What can I do?'

I said, 'Anything'.

So I went on sweeping. Sweeping all the alleys out, sweeping the gangway, keeping it all clean, picking up the waste.[385]

384 Memories of Flo Melhuish in *BRISTOL as WE remember it* (Bristol: Bristol Broadsides) pp. 10-11. I am grateful to Colin Thomas for this reference.
385 Memories of Flo Melhuish in *BRISTOL as WE remember it*, pp. 10-11.

Conclusion

So what can we conclude from this detailed study of labour and resistance among women as well as men at the Barton Hill cotton works? The opening of the Great Western Cotton Company would not have been possible without the existence of a powerful British Empire. Profitable markets for the export of textile goods and sources of raw materials had been made available to British businesses in the late eighteenth and early nineteenth century. Moreover, it would have been much less likely to get a modern cotton mill built in Bristol without the payment of lavish amounts of compensation from the state to Bristol-based slave-owners, and those who had gained financially in other ways from slavery.

The receipt of this 'blood' money had a significant impact on Bristol's economy as some Bristol merchants reinvested their compensation capital in Bristol's docks, railways and the Great Western Cotton Works.[386] In turn this boost to the Bristol economy helped to enhance the status and influence of these merchants in local and national politics, the church and charities, such as the Dolphin Society. Thus through wealth and influence, and making a virtue of local patriotism, some of these merchants came to be included in the list of eminent *Bristol Worthies*. Charles Pinney, Philip William Skinner Miles, Henry Bush and George Gibbs, four of the original partners of the great Western Cotton Company who had received either directly or indirectly slave-ownership compensation, were recorded in the 1907/1909 *Bristol Worthies* series. Pinney was described as 'deservedly respected by all who had the pleasure of his acquaintance'.[387]

However, the key factor in sustaining the Great Western Cotton Works for several decades was the labour power supplied by female and male cotton operatives, the creators of cotton products. These operatives had little say or influence over their working conditions. Moreover, up to 1875, employees could be prosecuted and punished under criminal law for breaching their contracts of employment. By keeping wages low and paying scant concern for the health and safety of its workforce the company was able to make a profit, reward its managers with generous salaries and pay dividends to its shareholders. Children, who were employed in large numbers in the cotton industry, were frequently bullied and beaten. Women and girls in particular were treated with contempt.

---

386 Draper, *The Price of Emancipation: Slave-ownership, Compensation and British Society at the End of Slavery*, p. 257.

387 A. B. Freeman, *Bristol Worthies and Notable Residents: Past and Present* (Bristol: Burleigh, 1st Series, 1907), p. 63; For Bush and Miles see Freeman, *Bristol Worthies and Notable Residents: Past and Present* (Bristol: Burleigh, 2nd Series, 1909).

All of the operatives worked in constant danger of sustaining injury from a work related accident.

Notably, however, the state stepped in with Factory legislation aimed to eliminate the worst company practices such as unfenced machinery, ensuring mandatory education for children under the age thirteen, limiting the working hours of children aged between nine and thirteen and barring children under the age of nine from working in textile mills. Unsupported by a majority of manufacturers the passing of the Factory Acts reflected on the one hand concern about the possibility of increasing social unrest and on the other pressure and petitions from textile operatives in Lancashire and Yorkshire supported by the Tory radicals such as Richard Oastler and Michael Sadler, and a little later the Chartist movement.

Though welcome, the Factory Acts, however, failed to make a significant impact in reducing industrial accidents as illustrated by their regular occurrences throughout most of the nineteenth century at the Great Western Cotton Works and indeed elsewhere.[388] And the responsibility for these accidents was rarely placed on the employer. Moreover, little or no attention was given to attending to occupational diseases. It was to be the end of the nineteenth century before the national government recognized the need to regulate even the most dangerous trades.

Consideration of the privations of factory women had to wait until 1893 when, after decades of campaigning, the first two female factory inspectors were appointed; a step in the right direction but hardly enough to ensure that the needs of factory women. Factory inspectors focused 'on factors affecting general health, such as ventilation, long hours, inadequate meal breaks and inappropriate toilet facilities.' [389] They were able to expose cases of cruelty. In 1899, they found one twelve-year old girl employed in a spinning mill who had been repeatedly beaten 'deformed, undersized, knock-kneed, her feet turned inwards, thin and pale-faced'.[390] However, as Helen Jones argues the 'appointment of women inspectors helped to maintain women's working conditions as an 'apolitical' issue.'[391]

388 Though, by 1880, extensively covered by the Factory Acts, legislation did little to prevent factory workers sustaining 'a significant harvest of injuries, disabilities and deaths through accidents at work.' A. J. McIvor, *A History of Work in Britain 1880-1950* (London: Palgrave, 2001), p. 119.
389 H. Jones, 'Women Health Workers: The Case of the first Women Factory Inspectors in Britain', *The Society for the Social History of Medicine* 1:2, 1988, p. 172.
390 Jones, 'Women Health Workers: The Case of the first Women Factory Inspectors in Britain', pp. 178-9.
391 Jones, 'Women Health Workers: The Case of the first Women Factory Inspectors in Britain', p. 180.

So despite the Factory Acts, and the subsequent prosecutions, employers either disregarded, or sought ways in which to avoid complying with factory legislation. By the turn of the century it cannot be said that the working conditions of workers in the textile industry had changed significantly for the better. However, Bristol's cotton operatives, especially the women weavers, had constantly battled against the diminution of pay and poor treatment. They did not always sit around waiting for the law to come to their assistance. When pushed to their limits they found disparate ways, including strikes, of making a stand against the unreasonable commands of their uncompromising and malevolent employer.

Although it took decades to materialize, one lesson they drew from their experiences was the benefit of becoming collectively organized into a trade union in the fight to obtain justice at work. However, partly because of the conservatism of the erstwhile militant Gasworkers' and General Labourers' Union, the tradition of Bristol's women cotton workers in taking spontaneous strike action continued up to the outbreak of the First World War in order to bring pressure to bear on their employer in cases that they deemed as particularly unwarranted, especially wage reductions. This discontent, however, did not lead inevitably to the politicization of the women, or indeed men, employed at the Barton Hill cotton works. Evidence of the emergence of political class-consciousness in East Bristol (the location of the cotton works), expressed through the ballot box, did not emerge until the early 1920s when the constituency became a Labour stronghold. Ironically this occurred in the same year that cotton production at the Great Western Cotton Works ended in 1923.[392]

392 Atterton, *Cotton Threads*, p. 22.

Appendix 1

(Bristol Record Office (BRO) 13423/30)

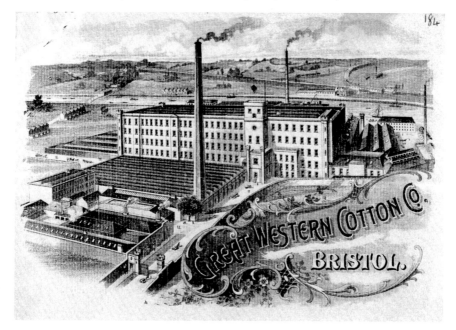

Private and Confidential

To the Workpeople.

The Directors have learned with great regret that a large number of the workers at the Cotton Works have again been guilty of the very serious offence of leaving work without proper notice.

Those who have acted thus have caused not only serious loss to the Company at the present moment through stoppage of the Works and the probable cancellation, owing to non-delivery at the time arranged, of orders on the Company's books, but have also inflicted a very great hardship on their fellow workers, who in consequence of their action have been deprived of their work.

The Directors would point out that such conduct is condemned by every Trade Union, and reasonably so, for if workers are to be at liberty to throw up their work at a moment's notice, it is obvious that the proper conduct of their business is impossible.

The Cotton industry in Bristol is carried on under great disadvantages, and the Directors are not prepared to continue the business if, added to their necessary anxieties and difficulties, they are to have this unreasonable friction with their workpeople. They have therefore decided in the interests of the Company and also in true the interests of the people themselves, that either these sectional strikes without notice must be stopped or that the Great Western Cotton Works must cease to be carried on.

It is not necessary to point out that if the latter alternative is forced upon the Directors a very heavy penalty will be paid by the wage-earning class of Bristol, since it will affect not only those actually employed at these Works, but also many others employed in other Bristol industries.

The Directors do not believe that the majority of the workpeople approve of these sectional strikes, but rather that they are caused by the impulsiveness of the younger and more irresponsible hands, and they therefore appeal to the common sense and reason of the majority to assist them in maintaining the proper discipline which is essential to the success of any enterprise, by sternly discountancing any stoppage of work without due notice.

The Directors would also call the attention of the workpeople to the fact that they have several privileges which are quite unusual, in the shape of holidays which are paid for by the Company, and they now give notice that for the future holidays will not be paid for if in the periods preceding them any portion of the Works shall have been stopped through workers leaving work without notice.

The Directors have thought it well that every one employed in the Works should be taken into their confidence, and should know what the inevitable result must be if the sectional stoppages without notice are not put a stop to, and for this reason they have issued this communication, so that hereafter if in consequence of these sectional stoppages the Works are closed, no one will be able to say that he or she, as the case may be, had not been put in possession of the facts, and had not had full and complete warning.

THE BOARD OF DIRECTORS
18th April, 1908.

Bibliography

Archives

British Newspaper Archive, (Findmypast Newspaper Archive Limited).

Census Returns of England and Wales, 1871, 1881, Ancestry.com, courtesy of the National Archives of the UK.

Daniell, M., Born H., and R. G. Tovey 'Reasons Why Tailoresses Should Join A Union, leaflet addressed to fellow workers', (January 1890), Tamiment Library/Wagner Archives, New York.

Great Western Cotton Company Partnership Deeds concerning the arrangement on the retirement of J. B. Clarke, Bristol Record Office (BRO).

Great Western Cotton Company's 'Letter' Book 1843-76, BRO.

Great Western Cotton Factory 'Dissected accounts' book, 9 October 1844 — 2 July 1845, BRO.

Minutes of the Bristol Workers' Organising Committee, Oct. 1889 – July 1892, Bristol Record Office, Bristol, UK.

Minutes of the First Yearly Conference of Delegates of The National Union of Gasworkers' and General Labourers of Great Britain and Ireland, 19-21 May 1890.

Parliamentary Papers, Government Publications, Official Reports and Registers

Annual Report of the Poor Law Commissioners, Vol. 1 (London: HMSO, 1835).

Death by accidents compensation, 1846 (560). A bill (as amended by the Select Committee) intituled, an act for compensating the families of persons killed by accidents, (House of Commons Parliamentary Papers online).

Elementary Education Act 1870 (London: Her Majesty's Stationary Office, HMSO), Chapter 75, Section 74, Clause 1.

Factories' Acts: 1833 (48) 3 Will. IV. —Sess. 1833, a bill to regulate the labour of children and young persons in the mills and factories of the United Kingdom, Clause 18 (House of Commons Parliamentary Papers online).

Factories' Acts: A return of the number and names of persons summoned for offences against the Factories Act, between 1 January 1843 and 1 January 1844, HOUSE OF COMMONS PAPERS; ACCOUNTS AND PAPERS, Paper No.106, Vol. XXXIX, P. 275, (House of Commons Parliamentary Papers online).

Factories' Inquiry Commission, 1834 (167). Supplementary report of the Central Board of His Majesty's commissioners appointed to collect information in the manufacturing districts, as to the employment of children in factories, and as to the propriety and means of curtailing the hours of their labour. Part 1, p. 179 (House of Commons Parliamentary Papers online).

Hansard, 24 March 1843 Vol. 67 cc 1411-77, Factories-Education: Sir James Graham.

Hansard, 30 July 1873, Vol. 217, cc 1287-1306: Henry Fawcett.

Hansard, 1 April 1890, Vol. 343, cc 399-400, Factory Acts-Great Western Cotton Works Bristol: R. B. Cunningham Graham.

Report by R. J. Saunders, 1844 (583) Reports of the inspectors of factories to Her Majesty's Principal Secretary of State for the Home Department, for the half-year ending 30th June 1844, (House of Commons Parliamentary Papers online).

Report of the Commissioners on Conditions in Factories (House of Commons Parliamentary Papers online), 1833, XX.

Reports of the inspectors of factories to Her Majesty's principal secretary of state for the Home Department for the half-year ending 30th April 1875 [C.1345], (House of Commons Parliamentary Papers online)

Reports of the inspectors of factories to Her Majesty's Principal Secretary of State for the Home Department, for the half-year ending 30th April 1846, 1846 (721), (House of Commons Parliamentary Papers online).

Reports of the inspectors of factories to Her Majesty's Principal Secretary of State for the Home Department, for the half-year ending 30th April 1847, 1847 (828), (House of Commons Parliamentary Papers online).

Senior, Nassau. Poor Law Commissioners' Report of 1834. London: H.M. Stationery Office. 1905.

Newspapers and Periodicals of the Time

Aberdeen Journal
Bath Chronicle
Bath Chronicler & Weekly Gazette
Bristol Mercury
Bristol Mirror
Bristol Times and Mirror
Felix Farley's Journal
Gloucester Journal
John Bull (London)
London Daily News

Manchester Courier & Lancashire General Advertiser
Morning Post
Northern Star
Taunton Courier & Western Advertiser
The Englishwoman's Review
The Shield
The Times
The Women's Union Journal:
    The Organ of the Women's Protective and Provident League
Western Daily Press
Worcestershire Chronicle
Yorkshire Post and Leeds Intelligencer

Books and Pamphlets

Atterton, G., *Cotton Threads: The History of the Great Western Cotton Factory* (Bristol: Barton Hill History Group, June 2015).

Bailey, V., 'The Fabrication of Deviance: Dangerous Classes' and Criminal Classes' in Victorian Britain' in J. Rule and R. Malcolmson (eds.), *Protest and Survival: The Historical Experience, Essays for E. P. Thompson* (London: Merlin, 1993).

Beckert, S., *Empire of Cotton: A New History of Global Capitalism* (London: Penguin, 2014).

Beven, T., *The Law of Employers' Liability and Workmen's Compensation* (London: Steven & Haynes, 1909, 4th Edition).

Bolin-Hort, P. 'Government Inspectors and the Regulation of Industry: On theProblem of True Enforcement of the Early British Factory Acts' in *Bringing in the Inspector: the Framing and Enforcement of the Early Factory Legislation in Britain, 1825-1900*, Working Papers on Childhood and the Study of Children (Stockholm: Department of Child Studies, Linköping University, 1996).

Bristol Broadsides (ed.) *BRISTOL as WE remember it* (Bristol: Bristol Broadsides)

Bronstein, J., *Caught in the Machinery: Workplace Accidents and Injured Workers in Nineteenth-Century Britain*, (California: Stanford University Press, 2007).

Bryher, S., *An Account of the Labour and Socialist Movement in Bristol.* (Bristol: 1929), Part 2.

Budd, W., 'Asiatic Cholera in Bristol in 1866', *British Medical Journal*, 13 April 1867.

Budd, W., 'Malignant Cholera: its cause, mode of propagation, and prevention' reprinted in the *International Journal of Epidemiology*, 2013: 42, pp. 1567-1574 (First published in 1849, London: Churchill).

Bulley A. A. and Whitley, M., *Women's Work* (London: Methuen, 1894).

Busbey, K. G., 'The Women's Trade Union Movement in Great Britain', *Bulletin of U.S. Dept. of Labor Statistics*, No. 83, July 1909.

Cannon, J., *The Chartists in Bristol* (Bristol: Bristol Branch of the Historical Association, 1964).

Charley, W. T., *Conservative Legislation for The Working Classes. No.1 Mines and Factories* (London, Westminster: The National Union of Conservative and Constitutional Association, 1885 (LSE Selected Pamphlets)).

Clark, A., *The Struggle for the Breeches: Gender and the Making of the British Working Class* (London: University of California Press, 1997, first published 1995).

Crossick, G., 'The Labour Aristocracy and its Values: A Study of Mid-Victorian Kentish London', *Victorian Studies*, Vol. 19 No. 3 (March 1976).

Dale, P., Greenlees J. and Melling, J., 'The Kiss of Death or a Flight of Fancy? Workers' health and the campaign to regulate shuttle kissing in the British cotton industry, c. 1900-52, *Social History*, Vol. 32:1.

Davey Smith, G., 'Commentary: Behind the Broad Street Pump: aetiology, epidemiology and prevention of cholera in mid-19th century Britain', *International Journal of Epidemiology*, 2002: 31: pp. 920-932.

Dix, G., *The Image Breakers* (New York: F. A. Stokes, 1909).

Drake, B., *Women in Trade Unions* (London: Virago, 1984, first published 1920 by the Labour Research Department).

Draper, N., *The Price of Emancipation: Slave-ownership, Compensation and British Society at the End of Slavery* (Cambridge: Cambridge University Press, 2013, first published 2010)

Engels, F., *The Condition of the Working Class in England in Karl Marx, Frederick Engels Collected Works* Vol. 4 (London: Lawrence & Wishart, 1975).

Farnie, D. A., *The English Cotton Industry and the World Market 1815-1896* (Oxford: Clarendon Press, 1979).

Frank, C., *Master and Servant Law: Chartists, Trade Unions, Radical Lawyers and the Magistracy in England, 1840-1865* (Aldershot: Ashgate, 2010).

Freeman, A. B., *Bristol Worthies and Notable Residents: Past and Present* (Bristol: Burleigh, 1st Series, 1907).

Freeman, A. B., *Bristol Worthies and Notable Residents: Past and Present* (Bristol: Burleigh, 2nd Series, 1909).

Freifeld, M., 'Technological Change and the 'Self-Acting' mule: A Study of Skill and the Sexual Division of Labour', *Social History*, Vol. 11. No. 3, October 1986.

Galbi, D. A., 'Through Eyes in the Storm: Aspects of the Personal History of Women Workers in the Industrial Revolution', *Social History* Vol. 21 No. 2 May 1996.

Gibson, C., *The Bristol School Board 1871-1903* (Bristol: Bristol Branch of the Historical Association, The University of Bristol, 1997).

Gillard D (2011) *Education in England: a Brief History* www.educationengland. org.uk/history.

Gray, R., 'The Aristocracy of Labour in Nineteenth-Century Britain c. 1850-1914' in L. A. Clarkson, *British Trade Union and Labour History: A Compendium* (New Jersey: Humanities Press International, 1990).

Greenlees, J., "Stop Kissing and Steaming!': Tuberculosis and the occupational health movement in Massachusetts and Lancashire, 1870-1918', *Urban History*, Vol. 32:2, August 2005.

Greenlees, J., *Female Labour Power: Women Workers' Influence in Business Practices in British and American Cotton Industries, 1780-1860*(Aldershot: Ashgate, 2007).

Guyton, G. P. 'A Brief History of Workers' Compensation', *Iowa Orthopaedic Journal*, Vol. 19, 1999.

Halévy, E., *A History of the English People in the Nineteenth Century Vol. 3* (London: Benn, 1961).

Hall, C., Draper, N., McCelland, K., Donington, K., and Lang, R., *Legacies of British Slave-ownership: Colonial Slavery and the Formation of Victorian Britain* (Cambridge: Cambridge University Press, 2014).

Hannam, J., "An Enlarged Sphere of Usefulness': The Bristol Women's Movement, c. 1860-1914' in M. Dresser and P. Ollerenshaw (eds.) *The Making of Modern Bristol* (Bristol: Redcliffe Press, 1996).

Hay, D. and Craven, P., 'Master and Servant in England and the Empire: A Comparative Study', *Labour/Le Travail*, 31, 1993.

Hoffman, W. G., *British Industry 1700-1950* (Oxford: Blackwell, 1955).

Jennings, H., *Societies in the Making: A Study of Development and Redevelopment within a County Borough* (London: Routledge & Kegan Paul, 1962).

Jones, H., 'Women Health Workers: The Case of the first Women Factory Inspectors in Britain', *The Society for the Social History of Medicine* 1:2, 1988.

Jones, S., 'The Cotton Industry in Bristol', *Transactions and Papers* (Institute of British Geographers), No. 13 (1947).

Joyce, P., *Work, Society & Politics: The Culture of the Factory in Later Victorian England* (London: Methuen, 1980).

Kapp, Y., *The Air of Freedom: The Birth of the new Unionism*, (London: Lawrence & Wishart, 1989).

Kelly, J., *Rethinking Industrial Relations: Mobilization, Collectivism and Long Waves* (London: Routledge, 1998).

Kirby, P., *Child Workers and Industrial Health in Britain, 1780-1850* (Woodbridge, Suffolk: Boydell Press, 2013).

Kirk, N., *The Growth of Working Class Reformism in Mid-Victorian England* (Beckenham, Kent: Croom Helm, 1985).

Knott, J., *Popular Opposition to the 1834 Poor Law* (London: Croom Helm, 1986).

Kumar, R. 'Women in the Bombay Cotton Textile Industry, 1919-1940' in S. Rowbotham and S. Mitter (eds.) *Dignity and Daily Bread: New Forms of Economic Organising among Poor Women in the Third World and the First* (London: Routledge, 1994).

Kydd, A. S., *The History of the Factory Movement from the year 1802, to the Enactment of the Ten Hour Bill in 1847*, Vol. 1 (London: Simpkin, Marshall and Co., 1857).

Landes, D. S., *The Unbound Prometheus: Technological Change and Industrial Development in Western Europe from 1750 to the Present* (Cambridge: Cambridge University Press, 1987, first published 1969).

Lazonick, W., 'Industrial Relations and Technical Change: the Case of the Self-Acting Mule', *Cambridge Journal of Economics*, 1979, No. 3.

Lazonick, W., *Competitive Advantage on the ShopFloor* (Cambridge, Massachusetts: Harvard University Press, 1990).

Lewenhak, S., *Women and Trade Unions: An Outline History of Women in the British Trade Union Movement* (London: Ernest Benn, 1977).

Liddington J. and Norris, J., *One Hand Tied Behind Us: The Rise of the Women's Suffrage Movement* (London: Virago, 1978).

Lovell, J., 'British Trade Unions 1875-1933' in L. Clarkson (ed.) *British Trade Union and Labour History: A Compendium* (New Jersey: Humanities Press, 1990).

Marshall, P., *Bristol and the Abolition of Slavery: The Politics of Emancipation* (Bristol: Bristol Branch of the Historical Association, Pamphlet No. 37, 1975).

Marx, K., *Capital Volume 1* (London: New Left Review in association with Penguin Books, 1982, first edition published 1976).

McIvor, A. J., *A History of Work in Britain 1880-1950* (London: Palgrave, 2001).

Meller, H. E., *Leisure and the Changing City, 1870-1914.* (London: Routledge & Kegan Paul, 1976).

Midgley, C., *Women Against Slavery: The British Campaigns 1780-1870* (London: Taylor Francis, 2005).

Monaghan, J. J. 'The Rise and Fall of the Belfast Cotton Industry', *Irish Historical Studies*, Vol. 3, No. 9 (Mar., 1942).

Morgan, C. E., 'Women, Work and Consciousness in the Mid-Nineteenth-Century English Cotton Industry', *Social History*, Vol. 17, No. 1 (Jan. 1992).

Morris, M. D., *The Emergence of an Industrial Labour Force in India: A Study of the Bombay Cotton Mills, 1854-1947* (London: Cambridge University Press, 1965).

Munden (ed.), A. *Religious Census of Bristol & Gloucestershire 1851*, Vol. 29 (Bristol: The Bristol & Gloucestershire Archaeological Society, 2015).

Munro Smith, G., 'Cholera Epidemics in Bristol in the Nineteenth Century', *The British Medical Journal*, 10 July 1915.

Musson, A. E., *The Growth of British Industry* (London: Batsford, paperback edition, 1981).

Nardinelli, C., 'Child Labor and the Factory Acts', *The Journal of Economic History*, Vol. 40, No. 4 (Dec. 1980).

Owsley Jr., F. L., *King Cotton Diplomacy: Foreign Relations of The Confederate States of America* (Chicago: The University of Chicago Press, 1959).

Parry, Sir D. H., *The Sanctity of Contracts in English Law* (London: Stevens & Sons Ltd, published under the auspices of the Hamlyn Trust, 1959).

Pinchbeck, I., *Women Workers and the Industrial Revolution 1750-1850* (London: Frank Cass, 1969, first edition published 1930).

Ramelson, M., *The Petticoat Rebellion: A Century of Struggle for Women's Rights* (London: Lawrence and Wishart, 1972).

Richardson, M., 'The Bristol Strike Wave of 1889-90: Socialists, New Unionists and New Women: Part 1 and 2: Days of Hope' in D. Backwith, R. Ball, S. E. Hunt and M. Richardson (eds), *Strikers, Hobblers, Conchies and Reds: A Radical History of Bristol 1880-1939* (London: Breviary Stuff Publications, 2014).

Richardson, M., *The Enigma of Hugh Holmes Gore: Bristol's Nineteenth Century Christian Socialist Solicitor* (Bristol Radical History Group, 2016).

Rose S. O., 'From Behind Women's Petticoats": The English Factory Act of 1874 as a Cultural Production', *Journal of Historical Sociology* Vol. 4 No. 1 March 1991.

Rose, M. E., *The Relief of Poverty 1834-1914* (London: Macmillan, 1972).

Rothstein, T., *From Chartism to Labourism: Historical Sketches of the English Working Class Movement* (London: Lawrence and Wishart, 1983, first published in 1929)

Sanigar, W., *Leaves of a Barton Hill Notebook* (Bristol: University Settlement, 1954).

Simon, B., *Studies in the History of Education, 1780-1870* (London: Lawrence & Wishart, 1960)

Smith, G. Munro, 'Cholera Epidemics in Bristol in the Nineteenth Century', *The British Medical Journal*, 10 July 1915.

Talbot, M., A Plea for Women's Trade Unions, Pamphlet, Bristol, 1892.

Thackrah, C. T., *The Effects of the principal Arts, Trades, and Professions, and of civic states and habits of living on Health and Longevity* (London: Longman, Rees, Orme, Brown, & Green, 1831).

Thompson E. P., 'Time, Work-Discipline and Industrial Capitalism' in E. P. Thompson, *Customs in Common* (London: Merlin, 1991).

Thompson, D., *The British People 1760-1902* (London: Heinemann Educational, 1969).

Thompson, D., *The Chartists: Popular Politics in the Industrial Revolution* (Aldershot: Wildwood House, 1984).

Thompson, E. P., *Whigs and Hunters: The Origin of the Black Act* (London: Allen Lane, 1975).

Thornton J. and Pearson P., 'Bristol Water Works Company; a study of nineteenth century resistance to local authority purchase attempts', *Water History*, 5 (3), 2013.

Tressell, R., *The Ragged Trousered Philanthropists* (London: Lawrence and Wishart, 1985, first complete edition, 1955).

Tucker, E., 'Review' of Jamie L. Bronstein, *Caught in the Machinery: Workplace Accidents and Injured Workers in Nineteenth-Century Britain*, (California: Stanford University Press, 2008), Le Travail, Vol. 62 (Fall, 2008).

Ure, A., *The Cotton Manufacture of Great Britain, Vol. II* (London: Charles Knight, 1936).

Ward J. T. and Treble J. H., 'Religion and Education in 1843: Reaction to the 'Factory Education Bill'', *The Journal of Ecclesiastical History*, Vol. 20, Issue 1.

Webb, S. & B., *History of Trade Unionism* (London: Longmans, 1920).

Webb, S. and B., *The History of Trade Unionism, 1666-1920* (London: Self published for the Students of the Workers' Educational Association, Christmas 1919).

Name Index

General Index